culture-proof kids

BUILDING CHARACTER IN YOUR CHILDREN

JEANNIE ST. JOHN TAYLOR

LIVING INK BOOKS
Writing Worth Reading™
Living Ink Books
An Imprint of AMG Publishers
CHATTANOOGA, TENNESSEE

Culture-Proof Kids: Building Character in Your Children

Published by Living Ink Books, an imprint of AMG Publishers
6815 Shallowford Rd.
Chattanooga, Tennessee 37421

ISBN 978-089957-116-4

First printing—April 2007

Cover designed by ImageWright, Chattanooga, Tennessee
Interior design and typesetting by Reider Publishing Services, West Hollywood, California
Edited and proofread by Mary McNeil, Barbara Martin, Dan Penwell, Rick Steele, and Rich Cairnes

Printed in the United States of America
13 12 11 10 09 08 07–V– 7 6 5 4 3 2 1

To my friends
Danny and Gloria Penwell

Other books by Jeannie St. John Taylor

The Guilt Free Prayer Journal for Moms, AMG
Prayers for Troubled Times, AMG
101 Stories of Answered Prayer, AMG
How to be a Praying Mom
What Do You See When You See Me? Illust. by Kathleen Kemly
Am I Praying
Am I Trusting
Am I Making God Smile
Am I Forgiving
How I Pray for My Friends
Erik's Christmas Gift Exchange
Who Did It?
Does God Have a Job?
God Loved Me so much He Created Me
Out at Home a youth novel about divorce
Matt's Fantastic Electronic Compusonic. Jeanne Gowen Dennis, illust. by Jeannie Taylor
You Wouldn't Love Me if You Knew
Together Forever
Penguin's Special Tree. Illus. Molly Idle

Jeannie answers all her emails personally and would love to hear from you. Contact her on her Website: www.jeanniestjohntaylor.com

Find the children's books that Jeannie St. John Taylor has written and illustrated at your local Christian bookstore, general bookstore, the Internet, or on her Website: www.jeanniestjohntaylor.com.

Contents

Acknowledgments

MY GREATEST delight in writing *Culture-Proof Kids* came as I searched the Scriptures each morning. I'm thrilled with God's Word every time I open it. Often I find myself pressing its pages to my chest and asking the Lord to make it sink into my heart and mind and become a part of me. I long to be a living, breathing version of God's Word. The most difficult task I faced came each time I had to stop quoting Scripture and add my own words—so weak in comparison with the great truths of the Bible.

My second greatest pleasure came from remembering my family as I wrote. God has blessed Ray and me with godly grandmothers, parents, and siblings; and we've been able to share that godly heritage with our children. Ray and I are so grateful all three of our children—Tyrone, Tori, and Tevin, and daughter-in-law, Kirsten—are people of character who love the Lord. Third John states that the apostle's greatest joy came from knowing his children were living in the truth—I agree wholeheartedly.

My list of blessings goes on to include: the editors who smoothed the bumps in my manuscript—Dan Penwell, Mary McNeil, and Barb Martin—all three of whom are close friends.

Trevor Overcash tended to myriads of details that polished the book. And the support people at AMG Publishers have always been so accepting and supportive—Dale Anderson, Rick Steele, Joe Suter, Warren Baker, Karen Moreland, Gin Chasteen, Donna Coker, and Amanda Donnahoe. My deep thanks to every one of them.

After finishing the edits on this book, one of the editors called and strongly suggested I find people who would begin to pray right away for you—the reader. I was able to tell her that a number of godly women had been praying for months already. I believe those women praying and I are a team that exemplifies the way the body of Christ is supposed to function. They love you, I love you, and we believe you can raise godly children. Please e-mail me with your concerns, and we'll partner in prayer with you.

Preface

THE CONCEPTS I share in this book took shape over time because I was, as the apostle Paul said of himself, "the worst of sinners." I had no common sense, no idea how to parent, and a very faulty sense of right and wrong. I was forced to turn to the Bible for help.

The precepts I found there served me well. My three children have grown into people of character. However, lest they appear perfect in my writings, please know they are not. I have mentioned few of their flaws because I don't feel I have the right to hold them up to public scrutiny. But believe me, they are flawed—just like your kids.

As you read, understand that as I look through this book there are many chapters that make me wish I'd done a better job of parenting. So don't feel condemned if you see your own failures at times. Just thank the Lord for helping you understand ways to parent more effectively and let the guilt go.

Jeannie St. John Taylor

Introduction

FOR FORTY YEARS, God's children had no home, no land, no houses, not even a place to grow crops for food. They wandered through a desert, living in tents they packed up and hauled to a new location every few days or months. Modern society has a name for people who live like that: homeless.

And yet, years later King David would maintain that the Israelites did have a home during those bleak years. In the psalms, he named that home: "Lord, through all the generations *you* have been our home!" (Ps. 90:1, author's emphasis). The word for home in that verse, *maw-ohn*, means "an abode, a retreat, a habitation" (number 4583 in *The New Strong's Exhaustive Concordance of the Bible*). Home for God's people wasn't a physical *place*, but it was a *Being* who was a retreat and an abode, a *Being* who offered security and provided for needs.

Though God's children waited forty years to build houses of stone on solid ground, God never left them homeless. *He was home.*

In much the same way today, God is home for Christians. He's a Father who loves his creation so much he provided human mothers and fathers who could imitate him, and become parents and, ultimately, a home. As parents raised their kids, God provided wisdom and a safe haven, helping them shape their children's character. It's a great mystery, seamlessly entwining hundreds of generations with the hand of the Holy.

Still, since even the best humans are flawed, our own parents inadvertently built flaws into us, and we need continually to ask God to restructure their work, bringing it closer to his standard of perfection. After we leave their home, he continues to repair our deficiencies and seal the gaps in our character. He repairs the structural damage we inflicted on our own spirits when we made bad choices.

While we're still unfinished and imperfect, he charges us with building character into our children. He commissions us to be home and parent. It's our responsibility, our joy, but it's also intimidating. Overwhelming. Thank God he doesn't abandon us; he never stops being our home as he builds us into home for our children.

It doesn't matter that our building skills are incomplete. As soon as we pick up the hammer and nails of love and discipline and ask for help, his hands cover ours, guiding them. He adds power to the impact of hammer on nail head, guiding the metal straight into the support beam in just the right direction. He knows so much more about constructing moral fiber than we do; wise parents ask for his assistance every step of the way.

Sadly, there are many parents who try to put together a home without the Master Builder's help. Those parents construct an empty house and children suffer. The Bible tells us, "Unless the LORD builds a house, the work of the builders is wasted" (Ps. 127:1). My dad's parents provide a good example.

My father's dad was an alcoholic who beat his wife, my grandmother. Everyone in the family, including my grandmother, insisted Grandpa was "one of the nicest guys you'd ever want to meet when he was sober." But he wasn't sober very often.

One night Grandpa came home drunk about three in the morning, and Grandma fled the house in near-zero temperatures. The kids were sleeping and she felt confident her husband wouldn't harm them, but she wouldn't be safe in the house. Since she had nowhere to go, she paced the snow-covered streets until morning in an attempt to stay warm.

Shortly after hurrying out the door, she heard footsteps crunching the snow behind her and turned to see my father, age five, following. Her heart broke. "Oh, Clare Duane, you can go home. Daddy won't hurt you, honey."

My dad lifted his tiny mitten-covered hands to his mother. "I want to stay with you, Mommy." He would rather spend the night walking frozen sidewalks than return to the house. Four walls and a bed didn't feel like home to my father; his sweet mom who loved the Lord—and him—was home.

Because my grandmother daily depended on the Lord, my father matured into a man of character and eventually became a pastor who joined with my mother to provide a solid home for my siblings and me. Even so, the Lord continued to work on my dad's character until the day he died.

Home is where character is forged—and one parent alone can do it with the Lord's help. A godly home is most likely to produce children of character.

So what does a solid home look like? How should a parent build a home for his or her children? The way God-our-Home treated his children in the wilderness presents a clear picture for us.

God proved he loved his children through his actions.

God disciplined them when they made wrong choices.

God comforted them.

God provided for physical needs by splitting open rocks and calling water to gush forth to satisfy their thirst; he sent manna from the sky in the mornings so they could eat. He kept them clothed; no shoes wore out during the forty-year trek.

God protected them from danger—enemies and wild animals.

God communicated with them through his servant, Moses, guiding them in the way to live successfully.

God remained faithful even though his children displeased him.

If we want to provide a home that will culture-proof our kids, we need to emulate God in each of those things. The purpose of this book is to offer practical suggestions for enlisting the Lord's help in accomplishing the goal of raising children of character. As you read, keep asking God to help you with this enormous task . . . because if you parent well, the rewards are immense.

"The father of godly children has cause for joy. What a pleasure to have children who are wise. So give your father and mother joy! May she who gave you birth be happy" (Prov. 23:24, 25).

1

Set a Foundation of Godly Principles

Thoughts become words
Words become actions
Actions become character
Character is everything.

ANONYMOUS

A Firm Base

Anyone who listens to my teaching and follows it is wise, like a person who builds a house on solid rock. Though the rain comes in torrents and the floodwaters rise and the winds beat against that house, it won't collapse because it is built on bedrock. But anyone who hears my teaching and doesn't obey it is foolish, like a person who builds a house on sand. When the rains and floods come and the winds beat against that house, it will collapse with a mighty crash.

MATT. 7:24–27

Because of God's grace to me, I have laid the foundation like an expert builder. Now others are building on it. But whoever is building on this foundation must be very careful. For no one can lay any foundation other than the one we already have—Jesus Christ.

1 COR. 3:10, 11

AN HOUR and a half from my Portland, Oregon, home are several houses that look like an illustration straight out of the Matthew 7 parable above. Every time a storm hits the coast, photos of its fury fill the front page of *The Oregonian* newspaper. Television news programs feature reporters buffeted by wind and rain, standing at a distance with cameras trained on the houses, speculating whether they will collapse, or if last-minute efforts to shore them up can save them.

Why? Those houses have weak foundations; foolish builders constructed them on sand.

When Jesus told the parable about houses built on sand he conveyed a spiritual principle; tragedy looms ahead for people who establish their lives on a weak foundation. Your children must have a solid foundation before they can stand firm when the storms of life assail. And you are the expert builder assigned by God to lay that foundation. If you're imperfect and feel wholly inadequate for the job, that doesn't change anything. The responsibility is still yours; if you don't do it, who will?

You must establish the character of your children on the Rock . . . Jesus Christ.

What Parents Can Do

- Pray, pray, pray. Never stop praying. Pray for wisdom and help for yourself daily; pray for supernatural protection for your children.
- *Know* God will help you. Believe it. He gave you a job you *can* do successfully—with his assistance.
- Take your children to church where they can become part of God's family. Insist they attend church. Ignore complaints. Tell them that while they live under your roof it's not up for discussion. A pattern of gathering together for worship was established by God in the Old Testament. In the New Testament, Hebrews commands that we "not neglect our meeting together" (Heb. 10:25). If you haven't found a church you and your children like yet, keep searching. Ask the Holy Spirit to guide you to the right one. (Hint: Look for a congregation where the attendees carry their Bibles.)
- Don't rely on Sunday school to teach your kids about the Lord; that's your responsibility. Tell your children Bible stories, and make certain they clearly understand God's concepts of right and wrong. Talk with them daily about Christian values. Do exactly as Deuteronomy instructs: "And you must commit yourselves wholeheartedly to these commands that I

am giving you today. Repeat them again and again to your children. Talk about them when you are at home and when you are on the road, when you are going to bed and when you are getting up" (Deut. 6:6, 7).

- If your children are getting older and you are just now starting to build a strong foundation for them, don't be discouraged. Be encouraged. There is always strong hope in God. He can work miracles if you trust him and pray, pray, pray.

Prayer for Myself

Guide me as I teach my children to love and obey you. Don't let me miss opportunities to speak about you with them so that you will be the firm foundation that keeps them safe and steady all through life.

Prayer for My Children

Jesus, become their Foundation, the Rock they can stand on in times of trouble.

Build on Solid Ground . . .

The Goal Is Love

Let love be your highest goal!

1 COR. 14:1

Above all, clothe yourselves with love, which binds us all together in perfect harmony.

COL. 3:14

May you experience the love of Christ, though it is too great to understand fully.

EPH. 3:19

AS PARENTS, we are obligated to teach our children about God and encourage them to follow him. But if we discipline or impart knowledge, even truths about God, with a negative spirit they will intuitively sense it, and our well-intentioned words may end up meaning something very different from what we intended.

No matter how we really feel about our children or what we say to them, if our attitude is wrong they will hear they are not valued, and their hearts will be wounded. They will feel unloved. Unworthy. They will have low self-worth.

Our main goal in parenting should be to make our children feel loved, accepted, and secure. If we do a good job of communicating love to our kids, they will naturally transition into an accurate view of God as loving and safe. Children who know they are loved are healthy children; children with good self-esteem are teachable. Children who know they are loved understand how to show love to others.

The world needs children like that.

What Parents Can Do

- Ask God to fill your heart with loving feelings every day.
- Since love is an action:
    - Spend lots of time with your children; nothing can replace time.
    - Give them abundant innocent physical affection. If you aren't a hugger, take hugging lessons from them. And smooching lessons. Kids need affection.
    - Say "I love you" every day.
    - Any time you think of something specific you appreciate about them, tell them about it in detail. Write it in a note and stick it in a drawer or in their lunchbox.
- Don't let them get away with misbehaving. Believe it or not, boundaries spell love to kids.
- Rid yourself of negative attitudes and feelings before you correct your children. God disciplines us in love, and your children deserve no less from you.
- Make sure they feel loved before you attempt to teach them anything. Josh McDowell wrote, "Rules without relationship (love) equals rebellion."
- If you're having trouble seeing anything good in them (this can happen in the teen years), spend time in prayer, asking God to give you wisdom and help you see them as he does.
- Speak twenty positives for every negative thing you are forced to say.

Prayer for Myself

Lord, sometimes I am not as loving as I should be. I think negative thoughts and I hold a lot of wrong attitudes. Heal me by letting me experience your love. Teach me how to communicate your love to my kids.

Prayer for My Children

Help them understand that I love them deeply even when I fail to show it as I should.

Build on Solid Ground . . .

God's Simple Plan for Parents

You are permitted to understand the secrets of the Kingdom of Heaven, but others are not. To those who listen to my teaching, more understanding will be given, and they will have an abundance of knowledge.

MATT. 13: 11, 12

No, the wisdom we speak of is the mystery of God . . . he made it for our ultimate glory before the world began.

1 COR. 2:7

BEFORE GOD created the world, he planned everything down to the minutest detail. For the most part, his plan is ineffable in its intricacy and remains a mystery to humans, though he allows his followers brief glimpses into the wonder of it.

Paradoxically, it can be beautiful in its simplicity, and God's plan for parenting is one of the simple aspects of his mysteries. He had to make it easy so we mortals could succeed. It would have been foolproof and effortless if humankind hadn't fallen, but it still works. The closer you can stick to his plan, the easier your job will be and the less trouble your children will have or cause you.

The plan is fourfold and works best for parents who search for and obey the Lord. Parents must:

- Know the difference between right and wrong and desire right.
- Consistently model righteous character.
- Set boundaries that fit the pattern of godly character.
- Implement consequences every time children step over those boundary lines.

It's a simple plan, and it's easy to see how well it can work. Even though it is impossible for any human to follow the plan perfectly, because we are all flawed, there are ways we can get closer and closer to doing it correctly.

What Parents Can Do

- If you get confused when trying to figure out if an action is right or wrong, start reading your Bible. Eventually, all your questions will be answered as you go to the Word consistently and ask the Holy Spirit to help you understand what you are reading. In the meantime, when a question you can't answer arises, instead of making quick decisions, seek out a wise Christian friend or a pastor to help you. Keep reading, because if you don't eventually progress to the point that you fully understand right from wrong, your children are headed for difficulties.
- If you desire to model godly behavior, pray and ask the Lord to help you accomplish it. Every time he points out something you need to change, determine to do as he says. Then refuse to keep beating yourself up for the mistakes you made. You may need a praying friend or a counselor who can help you work through past pain.
- If you are not modeling the kind of behavior your children should emulate, find a godly family in your church and ask if your children can spend time with them occasionally. If your children are never able to observe righteous behavior in

action somewhere, they will never know how to achieve it for themselves.

- To help you set and enforce boundaries, draw an outline in the shape of a heart. Keep the heart a light color; shade the area outside the heart and boldly write "unhappiness" and "disaster" at the outer edges of the darkness. List words describing bad character in the dim area close to, but just beyond, the lines of the heart. The words should list ways you don't want your children to behave. Begin with words from early childhood (temper tantrums, hitting siblings, shouting "Mine!"), proceed through elementary school (cheating on tests, "forgetting" homework, speaking disrespectfully), and continue into young adulthood (missing church, treating others badly, immorality). Inside the shape, where you want your children to live, are the words "noble character" and "successful life." Let the drawing remind you that if you allow your children to step across the boundary lines, they will. And just a nudge across that line is already in the area that leads to unhappiness and disaster. As long as they live under your roof and eat your food, it's your job to keep them inside the safety of the heart's boundaries, no matter how hard they fight you.

Prayer for Myself

Give me the wisdom to set right boundaries and the courage to keep my children from violating them.

Prayer for My Children

Help them understand why I set boundaries, and soften their hearts so they want to do the right thing.

Build on Solid Ground . . .

Convictions and Beliefs

[Jesus said,] "But everyone who denies me here on earth, I will also deny before my Father in heaven."

MATT. 10:33

[As he faced death, Paul wrote,] I am not ashamed, because I know whom I have believed, and am convinced that he is able to guard what I have entrusted to him for that day.

2 TIM. 1:12 NIV

As the time drew near for him to ascend to heaven, Jesus resolutely set out for Jerusalem.

LUKE 9:51

THE QUESTION came up as our small group discussed Cassie Bernall and the Colorado school killings: "What would you do if someone held a gun to your head and asked you to deny Jesus? Would you answer as Cassie did, knowing you'd lose your life?"

I felt a rise of fervent certainty. "I would never deny Jesus. Never. I know I'd need his help to stand firm, but I also know he would help me."

I thought everyone in the group agreed until Lydia later confessed, "I'd say whatever was necessary to save my life . . . but I wouldn't really mean what I was saying." Though Lydia believed in God, she lacked the courage of her convictions.

Beliefs are not the same as *convictions.* A *belief* is something a person knows is true; a *conviction* is something an individual is willing to die for.

There are some things a person must be willing to die for in taking a stand for Christ. Jesus didn't say it was OK for Lydia to deny him as long as she didn't really mean it. He said if a person denies him on earth, he'll deny that individual in heaven. Period. And the only way into heaven is through Jesus. What would you die for? Do your children know that? Do they share your convictions?

What Parents Can Do

- Make a list of your convictions, and make sure you've communicated them to your children.
- When they are old enough, ask your children to write out their own list. Make sure they understand they could actually face dying for their convictions someday, and they must determine ahead of time they will do it.
- Help your children understand that being willing to die for convictions is very different from the terrorists' stance on deliberately martyring themselves to kill innocents. People of character never seek death, but they possess the courage to die when necessary for what is right and holy.

Prayer for Myself

Give me noble convictions and the courage to die for them if need be.

Prayer for My Children

Make my children courageous and willing to give their lives to honor you, Lord.

Depend on God and Yourself

He takes no pleasure in the strength of a horse or in human might. No, the LORD's delight is in those who fear him, those who put their hope in his unfailing love.

PS. 147:10, 11

But Moses told the people, "Don't be afraid. Just stand still and watch the LORD rescue you. . . . The Lord himself will fight for you. Just stay calm." Then the Lord said to Moses, "Why are you crying out to me? Tell the people to get moving! Pick up your staff and raise your hand over the sea. Divide the water so the Israelites can walk through the middle of the sea on dry ground."

EXOD. 14:13–16

HOW MANY times have you heard someone quote the scripture, "God helps those who help themselves"? I recently heard it on a television news report from a young woman who followed it with a direct look into the camera and an emphatic, "And that's the truth." She did admit she couldn't remember where the verse was located in the Bible, and here's why: It isn't in the Bible; it's a lie.

God doesn't ask his children to help themselves before he pitches in to assist with the final details. God created people to depend on him. He fights our battles, and we aren't required to lift a finger. As a matter of fact, he plans our rescue long before we see trouble.

God is the one who told Moses to lead the Israelites to the Red Sea with Egyptians in hot pursuit and mountains rising on either side. God left no escape route. When the Israelites panicked, Moses exhorted them to stand still and trust. God would fight the battle for them, Moses said, and they wouldn't have to do a thing in their own defense. He could confidently offer that assurance because he'd seen God do exactly that in the past. He knew it was true.

Yet nothing happened, and the Egyptians continued to advance. Moses fell on his face crying out to the Lord, and God's response may be the source of the false "scripture" above. God listed two specific actions Moses needed to take before God could rescue them: Get the people moving and stretch out his staff. Simple enough.

God intended to split open a sea and hold back an army to save his people—both great miracles beyond the capabilities of any human—but he could do it only if Moses and the people did their part by walking through it. That's the sense in which they "helped themselves."

Here's the balance: We must have complete confidence in God; he created a plan for our lives before we were born and he will help us succeed. He *will* fight our battles. But we must have complete confidence in ourselves and in our ability and authority to do whatever God assigns.

What Parents Can Do

- Impress on your children the necessity of depending on God. They can't live without him because he created them to need him. Trying to do so without his help is like refusing to feed their bodies or plug in the computer. He's the power source.

- Tell your children God has a plan for their lives. He has gifted them for the job he wants them to do. He already laid the groundwork and will open doors. All they have to do is trust him and do their best. They "help themselves" by working hard at whatever they do, learning about the Lord and serving him. They must believe they can do it.
- Talk about ways they can keep doing their part; this will differ at various ages.
- When they're young and want friends, they should ask God for help, and then treat others in a friendly manner.
- For a good grade, they can ask God to help on a test but do their part by studying.
- Later if they need a job, they should ask God to guide them and open doors, but they must also contact potential employers.
- Instruct your children that there are times we do nothing and deserve nothing, and yet the Lord is gracious to open doors and surprise us with blessings. Still, if they've been praying and praying and the Lord isn't answering, one reason may be their own inaction. Are they asking God for something they are capable of doing? It is possible for inaction to hinder God's plan for them.

Prayer for Myself

I'm so grateful I can trust you to fight all our battles for us. Help me communicate this truth to my children.

Prayer for My Children

Help them trust you while maintaining confidence in their own authority and ability to do the job.

Know God Is Watching

O LORD, you have examined my heart and know everything about me. You know when I sit down or stand up. You know my thoughts even when I'm far away. . . . I could ask the darkness to hide me and the light around me to become night—but even in darkness I cannot hide from you.

PS. 139:1, 2, 11, 12

He knows everything—doesn't he also know what you are doing?

PS. 94:10

For he looks throughout the whole earth and sees everything under the heavens.

JOB 28:24

Your Father, who sees everything . . .

MATT. 6:4

For God watches how people live; he sees everything they do. No darkness is thick enough to hide the wicked from his eyes.

JOB 34:21, 22

AS A YOUNG child, my father wondered if he could hide from God under the patchwork quilt on his bed. Could God see him if it was dark outside and he tucked the cover tightly around himself ? What about back in the corner of the shadowy basement behind the coal bin? Could God see him there? Was there anywhere he could hide from God, or did God see every bad thing he did?

No doubt many people—both children and adults—wonder about that. That's why God answered the question in the verses above. There is nowhere to hide from God. He sees every detail of every person's life. He saw your children in the womb and has watched them ever since. He reads their thoughts when they feel angry or afraid. He hears every kind comment or nasty word they utter.

Realizing he sees everything—the good and the bad—can be a little frightening to children and adults. How could God love them after all the awful things they've done?

I wrote and illustrated a book on that topic called *You Wouldn't Love Me If You Knew* (Abingdon). My church sells it in the Resource Center, and the women who work there tell me they've seen adult after adult cry as they read that simple children's book. Tears flow because those dear people know God sees everything they do, and they know they've done a lot of ugly things. The book assures them of something they have trouble believing: Even though God actually witnessed those things, he loves and forgives them.

What Parents Can Do

- Teach your children the word *omniscient,* which means "all-knowing." Help them understand only God is omniscient. No other being on earth or in the heavens has that power—not moms and dads, not angels, not the devil.
- Spend the majority of the time on this subject saying how pleased you are when they choose goodness. Let them know you believe they choose right more often than wrong. Tell them it delights God, too.

- Remind them he sees the nice things no one else will ever know about, and he'll reward them in heaven. Doing precious things that only God can see is like hiding a secret treasure to use later.
- Train them to understand that because God already knows everything about them, he's aware when they're in trouble and he'll be waiting to help. Still, they need to whisper a prayer to ask for it.
- Impress on your children that though God sees every awful thing they do, hears every mean word they speak, and reads every naughty thought, he loves them anyway and will always forgive them when they ask. If they comprehend that as children, they'll never need to cry as grown-ups when they read a book like *You Wouldn't Love Me If You Knew.*
- Stress the importance of being constantly aware that God sees the details of their lives. Help them understand how much it hurts God when they choose wrong. If they love God, knowing it grieves him when he has to watch them sin will prevent a lot of problems.

Prayer for Myself

It takes my breath away that you know everything about me and love me anyway. Thank you.

Prayer for My Children

May knowing you are always watching and protecting them give them great joy and comfort.

Develop a Strong Identity

O Sovereign LORD, you told your servant Moses that you had set Israel apart from all the nations of the earth to be your own special possession.

1 KINGS 8:53

I will be their God, and they will be my people. Therefore, come out from among unbelievers, and separate yourselves from them, says the LORD.

2 COR. 6:16, 17

Don't you realize that all of you together are the temple of God and that the Spirit of God lives in you? . . . For God's temple is holy, and you are that temple.

1 COR. 3:16, 17

You must be holy because I am holy.

LEV. 11:45

I REMEMBER the unsettling call from Tevin's third-grade teacher. The school counselor had administered a psychological profile evaluation to the entire student body, and teachers were "very concerned" about Tevin's results. Though they stated their fears diplomatically over the phone, I could tell they viewed that test as a predictor of maladjusted future serial killers. Since I live next door to the school and volunteered regularly, I made it to the counselor's office in less than five minutes. She wanted to share results and worries; I asked to see the questions and Tevin's answers so I could evaluate it for myself.

In answer to whether he was "different" from others, Tevin had said "yes." That response, the very one that sent the school into a tizzy of anxiety, made me square my shoulders and smile with pleasure. Because from the time my children were old enough to gurgle in their cribs and listen to my voice I had been fervently telling them, "We are different; we are *Christians*. We always act like Jesus, even if it means we take a stand for right with everyone making fun of us. We treat others with kindness no matter what they do, because we are *Christians*. We belong to Jesus' family and he loves us."

So how did Tevin turn out? In junior high he literally stood to his feet, taking a position for righteousness with peers ridiculing him. He graduated from high school with a 3.7 grade point average and was voted "most athletic" his senior year. During college, he phoned his elderly grandfather every day, though he was busy running hurdles for track and earning a high average. Today he is married to a beautiful, committed Christian school teacher. At the end of this week he begins his third tour of duty in Iraq as a civilian engineer who maintains and operates unmanned spy planes for the military. Without the men who operate those drones, many more lives would be lost in the war. He does that job for his wife and country and because he knows who he is: a Christian who wants to please the Lord.

What Parents Can Do

- Give your children a strong *sense of identity*. Make sure they understand they are set apart—special, important, valuable—because they belong to Jesus. Belonging to Jesus is the one thing God's Word says we not only *can* but *should* feel pride about. We're supposed to boast about the cross.

- Give them a strong *sense of family*. Even if your own family is fragmented, they are members of the body of Christ, his beloved children (see Eph. 1:5). Read the twelfth chapter of Romans together and talk with them about their place in the body of Christ.
- Give them a strong *sense of responsibility*. They have a job as ambassadors of the Lord—now. They don't have to wait until they get older. Their actions reflect on Christ. When others observe the conduct of your children, they will either form a good opinion of Jesus because of your children's good behavior or develop a bad opinion of him because of your children's bad behavior.
- Give them a *strong goal*, to "live for Christ, who died and was raised for them" (2 Cor. 5:15).

Prayer for Myself

Give me a strong sense of my identity in you, and show me how to communicate that confidence to my children. Show me how to cooperate with the Holy Spirit in inspiring them to choose you.

Prayer for My Children

Help them understand their position as your beloved children. Show them how much you love them and how valuable they are to you. Never let them doubt who they are. Instead of feeling ashamed of you, help them love boasting about Jesus.

Build on Solid Ground . . .

Prayer

I love the LORD because he hears my voice and my prayer for mercy.

PS. 116:1

In my distress I prayed to the LORD, and the LORD answered me and set me free.

PS. 118:5

You can ask for anything in my name, and I will do it, so that the Son can bring glory to the Father. Yes, ask me for anything in my name, and I will do it.

JOHN 14:13, 14

But the love of the LORD remains forever with those who fear him. His salvation extends to the children's children of those who are faithful to his covenant, of those who obey his commandments!

PS. 103:17, 18

The descendants of those who obey him will inherit the land, and those who love him will live there in safety.

PS. 69:36

AT NINE years of age my daughter traveled alone to Colorado with her premier soccer team. Before I agreed to let her go without me (we couldn't afford to send both of us), I asked several parents on the team to watch over her. They promised they would. After assigning her to a room with three of the nicest girls on the team, the coach called ahead to make certain the adult channels were turned off their television set. I thought we had control of the situation.

We didn't. When Tori flipped on the television, nude scenes no child should ever witness popped onto the screen. In panic she switched to another station and another—same thing on every channel. Finally, she flung herself facedown on the bed until another child rushed over and switched off the set.

Know when I found out about it? Last week. She's twenty-seven now, and I thought she told me *everything* back then.

Fortunately, the whole time she was gone I prayed diligently for the Lord to protect her. Did he answer that prayer? I think he did. He protected her mind and spirit, keeping her from permanent damage. While I would have preferred she never face something like that, it didn't do lasting harm. She didn't rebel in her teens, and today she is a committed Christian who calls herself a "woman of prayer."

We parents often think we're in control when we aren't; bad things happen in this evil world. But God is in control, and he anticipates every shocking disaster well ahead of time. Better yet, he can eventually work out those terrible things for the good of your children, but he's waiting on your prayers to open the way. Why do you think God promises so many things for the children of the godly? I believe prayer is a major factor; righteous people pray continually for their children.

What Parents Can Do

- It's your responsibility to pray for your children. It's not your mother-in-law's, not your friend's, not your pastor's . . . it's yours. You need to lift them to the Father every day, every time you think of them. If you aren't praying for your children, you are leaving them in danger, vulnerable to Satan's evil working. No one else will ever speak to the Lord about them with the love and intensity you do. They *need* your prayers. *Yours!* Desperately.

- What should you pray for? Though I've written two entire books on the subject, *How to Be a Praying Mom* and *The Guilt-Free Prayer Journal for Mothers,* I would suggest three main things:
    - Pray for them to accept Jesus as Lord of their life, because there is no other path to heaven.
    - Pray daily for physical and spiritual protection.
    - Ask the Holy Spirit to open your eyes to which character traits you should pray into them. Then pray.
- Believe in the power of prayer. Jesus said if you ask for anything within his will he *will* do it. That's a promise. Asking for specific things will allow you to recognize those answers.
- When your children come to you with a problem, turn to prayer for wisdom before you do anything else. Ask them to pray with you. When they understand you are a person of prayer, odds are good they will be, too.
- Be confident God listens when you whisper the names of your children along with requests to him. The book of Revelation shows that our prayers rise to heaven as incense and fill gold bowls around God's throne (see Rev. 5:8). If you are a Christian, you are one of the "saints" mentioned in that verse. Let it comfort you to know God hears the names of your children.
- Don't decide how God is supposed to answer. Simply tell him what you need and ask him for faith to believe he is working while you wait. Know with certainty he has the power to care for your children, and he loves them more than you do.
- Don't expect your prayer burden to lessen as your children grow older; it will increase. As you gradually relinquish control of their decisions and actions, you must increase your prayers. When you have absolutely no control, you can still plead with God for them. And he'll never leave them.

Prayer for Myself

Open my eyes to know how to pray for my children, and make me faithful in prayer. Any time you nudge me with one of their names, I will pray for them.

Prayer for My Children

Compel my children to become people who continually turn to you in prayer. Increase their faith to believe you always answer them. Give them confidence that when you say "no" or "wait" those answers will work for their good and develop them into people of character.

The Primary Relationship

Then make me truly happy by agreeing wholeheartedly with each other, loving one another, and working together with one mind and purpose.

PHIL. 2:2

And further, submit to one another out of reverence for Christ.

EPH. 5:21

THOUGH NOW cliché, the following statement is still true: The most important thing you can give your child is a good relationship with your husband or wife. So why is it that so many couples are nice to each other until the wedding vows are said, and then all bets are off?

I know one couple who loved each other passionately before they married, but afterward the verbal battles raged so violently their eleven-month-old son would crawl into the closet to escape. I guess they didn't understand that their baby needed to see his parents experience a loving relationship in order to feel secure. They didn't realize he was already learning how to treat his own wife by watching them.

I'd like to think most marriages aren't as distressing as the one described above, and maybe they aren't. Still, everyone fights at least occasionally. So what can be done to improve relationships?

What Parents Can Do

- If you don't know how to have a good marriage, look around for someone who seems to excel at it and ask if you can spend time with them. You'll pick up a lot of ideas and techniques.
- Don't be ashamed to seek counseling from a pastor or Christian counselor.
- No child feels secure if his or her parents are always fighting, so keep most arguments between the two of you.
- On the other hand, when children never see their parents fight, they may fear the marriage is falling apart when the parents have a small disagreement. So fight in front of them sometimes, but fight fair. (You may want to buy a self-help book or take a class to learn how to do that.)
- Spend time with your spouse. For nearly forty years, my sister and her husband have gotten up fifteen minutes early every day so they can sit together with a cup of coffee before they get dressed for work. I asked what happened when they were fighting. My brother-in-law told me there had been a few tense mornings, but they still stuck to their routine. They never stopped working at spending time together.
- Set aside a time to study the Bible together. My daughter-in-law tells me she and Tevin study the Bible together every evening after dinner.

Prayer for Myself

Teach me to be kind and loving to my spouse. Help me look for the good in him (her) instead of criticizing and accusing.

Prayer for My Children

Provide a strong Christian for them to marry, and teach them to be considerate and kind to each other.

Decide Who's in Charge . . .

Single Parenting

For your Creator will be your husband; the LORD of Heaven's Armies is his name! He is your Redeemer, the Holy One of Israel, the God of all the earth.

ISA. 54:5

Father to the fatherless, defender of widows—this is God, whose dwelling is holy.

PS. 68:5

I CAN'T imagine anything more difficult than single parenting. But just because single parents are without spouses doesn't mean they're without help. God loves single parents and their children, and he has promised to fill the role of both spouse and second parent for those who need him to do so. Not only will he fill the role, he'll do so perfectly!

My friend Kathi's husband abandoned her with two small boys. With God's help and a supportive family she raised a pastor and a Christian Division-1 athlete. My precious late pastor's mother raised him alone until she remarried. He turned out to be one of the godliest men I've ever known.

Both of my grandmothers functioned as single parents. My Michigan grandmother married an alcoholic who beat her and died at fifty-two, leaving her with a teenage son. My Kentucky grandmother's husband was a womanizer who worked in another state much of the time. Both women depended on the Lord to help them parent.

Between them, they raised two pastors, four pastors' wives, one Sunday school superintendent, and a missionary. They reared fourteen children in all, and every one was a Christian.

Trusting God may be difficult at times, but determine to do it. Remember that what you see with your eyes and hear with your ears isn't necessarily the truth. You are loved, even though your mate may have rejected you. God will keep his arms around your children even if they rebel and things look hopeless.

You can raise children of character despite the fact that you aren't married.

What Parents Can Do

- Don't give in to the temptation to live with someone you are not married to, and refuse to have sex without the benefit of marriage. If you are currently in one of those situations, extricate yourself immediately. Ask God for the courage and ability to do it, because it is urgent that you model God's laws for your children, and he forbids those things.
- Depend on the Lord and don't be afraid.
- Seek out godly role models for your children.
- If the absent parent has done terrible things to them or abandoned them, your children may fear they will become like that parent. I know a woman who used to cower under the stairs with her brother when their father arrived home drunk and brandishing a gun. It was important for her to learn that her Real Daddy loved her and would never choose to harm her. Teach them that God is their True Daddy (or Mama). They can be like their heavenly Parent instead of their earthly parent.
- Don't minimize any harm done to them; do not pretend it didn't happen. Instead, help them forgive (see the section on forgiveness in chapter 6). Then look for anything good in the parent who continues to hurt them.
- Lead them to pray for God to bless the absent parent.

Prayer for Myself

Thank you for being my spouse. Please give me the strength to trust you when I feel lonely and afraid. Help me to recognize any developing problems, admit them, and turn them over to you in prayer. Make us a family in you.

Prayer for My Children

Make them know they are loved. Reveal your loving heart to them. Give them contact with role models who will complete anything missing in their lives.

Blended Families

Since God chose you to be the holy people he loves, you must clothe yourselves with tenderhearted mercy, kindness, humility, gentleness, and patience. Make allowance for each other's faults, and forgive anyone who offends you.

COL. 3:12, 13

Fathers, don't scold your children so much that they become discouraged and quit trying.

COL. 3:21 TLB

IN HER BOOK *Raising Children in Blended Families* my friend Maxine Marsolini wrote of bulging suitcases carried home after the wedding that spill out with the smell of dirty laundry. "Tempers flare. Feelings are hurt. Tears flow. . . Instead of getting along, the children are competing, the parents are taking sides." It's a rare stepfamily that comes together effortlessly.

Rather, it's a difficult and potentially disastrous situation; sixty percent of second marriages end in divorce.

Maxine suggested it is urgent to *choose* to tuck your children into your heart and *let them know* about it, because God gave them to you, and "every time a blended family forms, it is built on the remains of the first family's broken dreams." Your children are grieving and they need you to help them heal. They need more love, tenderhearted mercy, kindness, humility, gentleness, and patience than ever before. And they need it from you.

What Parents Can Do

- Rather than feeling encumbered by your children, realize God has given you a gift, and practice being grateful for it. Every day tell him how much you appreciate your family. If you have to look in the mirror and say it out loud to believe it, do so. If you need to ask him to help you sincerely mean it, ask him.
- Since blended families require an extra dose of love, you need to continually go to the Source of love and ask for more. Though it will not be easy, he will enable you to overlook insults and hurts if you are determined to do it.
- Put the children and their feelings ahead of yourself and your feelings.
- Make an effort to treat all the children equally, and don't favor your biological children.
- Let the biological parent be the one to discipline, and then support him or her.
- Make sure you and your spouse spend time with your own children as well as your new children.
- Practice the Golden Rule. Work to understand how your children are feeling, and treat them the way you'd want to be treated. Work to make everyone feel valued.
- Don't try to keep the other biological parent from the children.
- Remember that things will get better. Maxine says it typically takes three to five years for blended families to feel like a solid unit.

Prayer for Myself

Shape us into a strong family unit. Teach me to love all my children deeply and enable me to love them in ways they understand so they will feel treasured. Guide my spouse and me to support and refuse to blame each other when things are difficult. Remind me to pray blessings for my spouse every day.

Prayer for My Children

Help them know I am not trying to replace their absent parent. Heal their grief, and help them fully understand that though we didn't start out as a family, we are a family now. And we love each other. Take away false guilt, and help them know they are not betraying their other biological parent by loving our family.

Decide Who's in Charge . . .

The Parental Core

Children, always obey your parents, for this pleases the Lord.

COL. 3:20

[Jesus] taught with real authority.

MARK 1:22

[The apostle Paul wrote to Titus,] You have the authority to correct them when necessary, so don't let anyone disregard what you say.

TITUS 2:15

GOD HAS given parents the job of turning their children into people of character while raising them with confidence and authority. Parents need to believe it and feel a certitude deep within that they can do the job. Dr. Paul Risser called it developing a "parental core."

He told about a bear he saw cowering high in a tree because it was afraid of a domestic kitty. Of course, the bear could have obliterated the cat with one swipe of its paw.

Some parents act just like that bear. They helplessly allow their two-year-old to hit them. They do nothing when their five-year-old shouts, "I hate you!"

Those things might happen *once* in any family. But if the parents know they are in charge and responsible for teaching their children, it shouldn't happen twice. God gave you children so you would teach them right from wrong and make sure they learn to submit to authority as they grow into responsible adults. God wouldn't give you a job you couldn't do. You must develop the deep conviction you can do it. When parents are strong in themselves and confident of what they must do, children sense it.

What Parents Can Do

- The motto of successful parents is "Show No Fear." If you push aside doubts and give the impression you feel confident, your children will trust your parenting skills and be more likely to obey you.
- If you are struggling to control your children, look in the mirror daily and say, "I'm in charge." Repeat it in an assertive voice until you believe it.
- Find parents who do a great job with their kids, and ask if you can hang out with them. Then copy what they do. That's how children learn from parents, and it's still one of the best ways for adults to learn. Why do you think universities require student teaching? So the young person can learn from an experienced teacher who knows how to do the job well.
- Colossians 3:20 says it pleases God when children obey; I think we can infer he is displeased when they disobey. If you want your children to please God, you must insist they obey you. No one else can do that for them.
- As they get older, you can gradually release the reins. But while they are young, you need to make the majority of decisions and then make sure they follow what you say. Without arguing.
- Explain to them the reasons for everything you do. Never say, "Because I said so." Even very young children need to hear your reasons so they can learn to reason things out.
- Never back down on something you know is right. Though at first glance it appears parents who give in to kids are very loving, they are actually behaving selfishly. Those parents care

more about what the children think of them than what is best for the children.

- Don't let yourself care if they get upset when you are making a decision for their well-being. God gave you the authority to decide those things for them because you have more experience and understand life better than they do.

Prayer for Myself

I *believe* I can do this job. Help me be strong. Give me a deep conviction that I can do it. Make me understand that you gave me the authority to successfully raise my children into productive adults.

Prayer for My Children

Make them obedient and pleasing to you. And to me.

Decide Who's in Charge . . .

Earn Respect

But if I didn't love others, I would have gained nothing. . . . Love never gives up, never loses faith, is always hopeful, and endures through every circumstance.

1 COR. 13:3, 7

JODI KINZINGER is an excellent third-grade teacher, one of the best I've seen—and I've observed lots of them. I won't mind if you accuse me of prejudice since she is my younger sister, but I've visited her classroom often enough that I can assure you I'm being objective.

The kids love her and obey her. Parents request her class well ahead of the third-grade year. Because of the way she treats students (she uses the same techniques with them she used on her own kids), Jodi has been able to build character in several problem students.

Casey is one of her success stories. In the first and second grades, students and teachers dubbed him the "Little Terrorist." In Jodi's third grade, his behavior changed radically. To reinforce that change, Jodi complimented him often, assuring him he wasn't the same boy in third grade he had been in first and second, and she was so proud of him.

Unfortunately, Casey tended to have temporary relapses when he was out of my sister's sight. One of these occurred near the end of a field trip when he used his juice container to machine-gun the back of the bus, leaving a wet, sticky mess.

"How did you handle it?" I asked her.

"I didn't do much. I called him to sit by me in the front seat."

"How'd he act?"

"He was instantly subdued; he's always good around me. I calmly asked him what he should have done. Then after all the other children exited the bus, I made sure he stayed to clean up."

Though teachers don't have the same influence on a child's character that parents do, my sister has done a lot to influence Casey's character . . . and his future.

So what exactly has Jodi done for him?

She genuinely loved Casey, even when he didn't deserve it, and he sensed it.

She treated him with respect by speaking calmly and matter-of-factly rather than losing her temper.

She continually told him the things she liked about him even though most people saw only the negatives in his character. (He in turn worked to prove her right.)

She held him accountable; he had to clean up the mess he made.

She focused time specifically on Casey.

What Parents Can Do

- Act in ways that prove you love and respect your children:
    - Because parents' words are often self-fulfilling, speak positively to your children whenever possible. Observe them carefully, and let them know every time they do something that makes you proud of them. Most of the things you compliment them for should deal with character issues and not achievements.
    - Tell the truth when you praise them. Don't commend them for something they didn't really do just to sound positive. Even the most ill-behaved child will demonstrate a good character trait if you wait long enough.

    - Be consistent in holding them accountable.
    - Instead of asking why they behaved in a certain way, ask what they should have done. It's an easier question to answer and looks at the situation with hope.
    - Be firm. If you treat your children with respect and *expect* them to respect you, they probably will.
- Start early. If you command respect when they are very young, you'll have a much easier time during the teen years. Conversely, if you fail to expect respect at a young age, your life and theirs will be miserable later.

Prayer for Myself

Help me treat my children with love and respect so they can learn those character traits from me.

Prayer for My Children

Help my children treat others—everyone from authority figures to classmates and friends—with respect.

Kids Want Rules

My son, obey your father's commands, and don't neglect your mother's instruction.

PROV. 6:20

Those who listen to instruction will prosper; those who trust the LORD will be joyful.

PROV. 16:20

BELIEVE IT or not, kids want rules. I discovered that strange truth as a twenty-something, teaching seventh and eighth graders in a rural Oregon town.

I can still see skinny Davis asleep at his desk, temple on his forearm, mop of straight brown hair flopping over his face. Everyone at school whispered about the marijuana. He didn't deny it. He didn't have to; he was the "cool kid."

Davis would rouse from his fog to shrug or mumble an "I dunno" whenever I directed a question his way, but he rarely volunteered to participate in class discussions . . . except for the day I took a vote in class. "Raise your hand if you want rules and you want your parents to enforce them." I thought maybe one lone student would have the courage to raise his or her hand. Maybe.

Instead, a large majority of the thirteen-year-olds immediately lifted hands indicating they did want discipline, including Davis. It shocked me. Who knew teenagers would admit to something like that in front of peers?

Still, what Davis did next surprised me even more. He sprang to life, pacing and gesturing as he spoke. He wanted rules and resented that his parents wouldn't discipline him. Oh, his mother would get mad and chase him with a broom occasionally, he said, but he pretty much got away with doing whatever he wanted. He admitted it made him feel as though his parents didn't care about him.

I consider that day one of the most astonishing of my twelve-year teaching career. I couldn't believe a teenager, especially the school's "cool kid," would share so openly. I always thought kids wanted boundaries and discipline somewhere deep in their psyches, but I had no idea they were aware of it.

Davis *knew* he wanted rules. But you can bet he never told his parents.

What Parents Can Do

- Boundaries make kids feel loved and secure, so set firm limits.
- Formulate your rules from God's Word, and let your children know they are his rules. They are responsible to him.
- Explain the purpose for your rules and invite discussion about them. That doesn't mean you give in. It's OK if the chat ends with your saying, "I understand your point of view. [Parrot their thoughts back to them here.] But God made me responsible to do what I think is right for you, and as long as you live in my house you still have to abide by my rules." If they have a good point, change the rule.
- Start early. Once kids reach Davis's age, they will fight all attempts to guide them, even if it is what they want down deep.

Prayer for Myself

Give me the wisdom to set boundaries and the courage to discipline my children when they cross them.

Prayer for My Children

Jesus, give them soft hearts and the willingness to submit to you.

Decide Who's in Charge . . .

Require Obedience

Rebellion is as sinful as witchcraft, and stubbornness as bad as worshiping idols.

1 SAM. 15:23

A wise child brings joy to a father; a foolish child brings grief to a mother.

PROV. 10:1

Discipline your children while there is hope. Otherwise you will ruin their lives.

PROV. 19:18

To discipline a child produces wisdom, but a mother is disgraced by an undisciplined child.

PROV. 29:15

EVERY TIME Julie left home in her Volvo, she dutifully buckled Amy into her child seat. Most parents understand why Julie did that: She loved her daughter and knew the car seat would protect her in case of an accident.

The problem was, Amy didn't understand, and Amy hated her car seat. So nearly every time Julie took her daughter anywhere, the toddler would click open the buckle and grin defiantly at her mother in the rearview mirror. She knew Julie wouldn't pull over on the freeway or a busy street. Julie "handled" the situation by scolding Amy as she drove. Amy ignored her.

The seeds of rebelliousness were planted.

Yvonne's toddler shared Amy's disdain for car seats. So he tried Amy's trick. When Yvonne pulled onto a busy street—*Click!*—Todd released the buckle. Without hesitating, Yvonne pulled to the side of the busy road and opened the back car door. With a sharp smack on Todd's bare leg, she fastened his seatbelt and positioned her face close to his. She made eye contact with him as she warned in her firmest mom-voice, "*Never* unbuckle your seatbelt again. *Never!*"

He never did.

Was Amy badly hurt in an accident, while Todd escaped injury? No. Both children grew to adulthood completely healthy—physically. Their spiritual health is another story.

Julie didn't make her daughter mind; Amy learned rebellion. She does not walk with the Lord today.

Yvonne required obedience; Todd learned to obey. He is a strong Christian today.

Is it possible that learning to obey parents teaches children to obey God? I think so.

What Parents Can Do

- Remember, you are a parent, not a friend. It's your job to quash any rebellion that pops up in your children.
- If your children misbehave, stop what you are doing so you can effectively deal with the problem, no matter how inconvenient or embarrassing it is.
- Don't be afraid to spank when words aren't enough to make them behave—especially when danger threatens.
- Teach your children that God made you their authority while they are young so they will know how to obey him as grown-ups.
- As they get older, gradually release them to God by letting them make their own decisions. Don't forget to remind them over and over they are ultimately responsible to God and he sees everything they do.

Prayer for Myself

Lord, help me love my children enough to require obedience from them. Teach me how to apply firm, loving discipline that refuses to accept rebellion.

Prayer for My Children

Keep my children from rebellion.

Decide Who's in Charge . . .

Discipline

> Don't fail to discipline your children. They won't die if you spank them. Physical discipline may well save them from death.
>
> PROV. 23:13, 14

> Those who spare the rod of discipline hate their children. Those who love their children care enough to discipline them.
>
> PROV. 13:24

SOMETIMES two-and-a-half-year-old Haze likes a wet "wipey" (paper towel), and sometimes he likes a dry one. So when he asked for one at lunchtime without specifying wet or dry, his mother decided to save herself some trouble and bring him one of each.

The problem was, she failed to do it precisely right. One of her wet fingertips touched the dry towel, leaving an unsightly raised spot. Haze couldn't stand it.

His mom handled the ensuing temper tantrum with aplomb. "Hazie," she said, calmly picking up the writhing monster, "I think you need a time out." She carried him to his room, set him down inside, closed the door, and set the timer for two minutes, one minute for each year of his life.

Within seconds she heard bangs and bumps and assumed Haze had taken off his shoes and hurled them against the wall in anger. She shrugged. She'd let him vent.

When the timer rang and she opened the door, the sight staggered her. Not only had Haze pulled all his covers and pillows off the bed and strewn clothes, toys, and shoes from his closet across the bedroom floor, he had managed to slather the whole mess with spit. In two minutes flat. He was just wiring up his mouth to hurl another wad when she entered the room.

Again Mom handled it well. Speaking calmly but firmly she said, "Well, I guess you're going to have to help me clean up this mess, Hazie."

He jutted out his lower lip, refusing to help. She insisted. Still, he resisted.

Going to the kitchen and retrieving the thin, white, plastic paddle from the electric grill found in most households these days, she swatted him. Twice. That was enough. He broke down in tears and started helping her clean up.

After they finished, she loved on him for a while and all was fine . . . till the next time.

What Parents Can Do

- Most—maybe all—kids require physical discipline at some point. Don't be afraid of it. Don't listen to advice or research that contradicts the Bible by saying spanking is harmful. God says you're going to have to spank sometimes if you love your children and want them to have character. He says it won't kill your kids. (See the verses quoted above.) He's never wrong.
- Don't spank while you are angry.
- Spanking should never leave red welts or bruises. That's called "beating," and the Bible never advocates that.
- Always hug and love on your kids after you discipline them. Make sure they know you love them no matter what they did.
- Although the Bible doesn't give an age limit for spanking, by age five you should be able to reason with a child or take away privileges when they choose to disobey.

Prayer for Myself

Give me wisdom to know when spanking is necessary. Help me love them no matter what they do, and show me how to communicate unconditional love as I discipline.

Prayer for My Children

Help them react in the right way to discipline.

2

Follow the Architect's Plan

"Education has for its object
the formation of character."

HERBERT SPENCER

The Bible Is Your Blueprint . . .

Make Right Choices

Your word is a lamp to guide my feet and a light for my path.

PSALM 119:105

CHOICES, CHOICES, choices. Is it better to spank, or to reason with children? Should parents place their kids in private school or let them be good examples for others to follow in the public system? Should children take piano lessons or play a sport? Or both? Is it a good or bad thing to sign them up for several activities at once? The world can be a confusing place for parents.

And it can be even more confusing for kids. What should they do if the school bully hits them? If they see a friend cheat on a test, do they tell or ignore it? Does it really matter if they take a candy bar off the shelf in the store without paying for it?

As they reach their teenage years the choices get more serious. Is it wrong to date a non-Christian if it won't lead to marriage? Is going to school dances OK? Even if there is drinking?

Throughout this book, I explain how my husband and I handled most of these questions with our children. But you don't have to take my advice; I know where you can find the right answers. All the questions you or your children ever have faced or will ever face are answered in the pages of the Bible, some directly and some indirectly. It takes a lot of effort, but they can be found and sorted through.

What Parents Can Do

Teach your children to consider the following before making any decision:

- Is it biblical? If you aren't well versed enough in the Bible to answer that question definitively, seek advice from someone who is.
- Will it help you grow and lead you the way the Lord is directing you?
- Are you able to say yes or no? If you're desperate to have it or do it, it may be wise to turn away, because your desperation proves that the thing you want has the potential to become more important to you than God. And that's called an idol.
- Is it wise? Or will there be a consequence? Sin always has a consequence.
- Will it affect your testimony? Will it make someone else stumble?
- Will you be spending a lot of time on something that has little value?
- Is it right? Sadly, many people choose to do things they know are wrong. Making right choices is the pathway to a full, satisfying life.

Prayer for Myself

Help me be an example of a person who understands what the Bible says to do and makes right choices. Give me wisdom to pass that skill along to my children.

Prayer for My Children

Teach them to seek wisdom from the Bible before they make a decision.

Color-Code Proverbs

Follow my advice, my son; always treasure my commands. Obey my commands and live! Guard my instructions as you guard your own eyes. Tie them on your fingers as a reminder. Write them deep within your heart.

PROV. 7:1–3

I USED PROVERBS as my parenting guide. After all, who better knows how to raise children than the God who made them? And most of his teachings can be found in abbreviated form in this collection of wise sayings from King Solomon and other wise men.

I discovered a simple way to organize the book and help my children "write the concepts deep within their hearts" after someone suggested color-coding for easy reference. I bought a box of colored pencils and started underlining. I underlined verses about lying in blue, work (laziness) in yellow, companions (friends, spouses) in orange, kindness and loyalty in pink, and money (poverty and wealth) in green.

Then any time a problem lifted its ugly head, my children and I would turn to Proverbs. If someone had not done homework, we'd look at yellow verses; if one had lied, we'd check out the blue verses. Sometimes I'd ask them to copy down several verses in the appropriate color or memorize one; other times we'd simply discuss the problem and what God had to say about it.

When my older son graduated from high school, his senior quote in the yearbook was one of the verses he had color-coded and subsequently memorized as a young child: "Listen to advice and accept instruction, and in the end you will be wise" (Prov. 19:20 NIV).

If you encourage your children to write God's advice deep within their hearts, those teachings will guide and comfort them the rest of their lives.

What Parents Can Do

- Tell your children how practical Proverbs is, and encourage them to read it. Show them how to read the chapter that corresponds with the day's date. Since there are thirty-one chapters, a good goal would be to read the entire book once a month. Tell them not to get down on themselves if they miss a day or a week.
- Color-code the book of Proverbs in your own Bible.
- Over time, a few verses and one subject at a time, go through Proverbs with your child, helping him or her color-code the appropriate verses in his or her own Bible.
- Encourage discussion about God's concepts and rules as you color-code. Explain to your children the wisdom of following what God says. Explain how you've set rules for yourself and them from God's Word.
- When a specific attitude or behavior problem pops up, use your color-coded Proverbs to quickly find several verses that teach about the issue.
- During your daily reading, color-code not just Proverbs, but other books of the Bible, too.

Prayer for Myself

Help me teach my children the importance of your teaching. Show me how to make obeying you very practical for them.

Prayer for My Children

Engrave your advice deep into the hearts of my children so those teachings will be with them their whole lives.

Discern Wisdom and Foolishness

Wisdom will multiply your days and add years to your life. If you become wise, you will be the one to benefit. If you scorn wisdom, you will be the one to suffer.

PROV. 9:11, 12

Love wisdom like a sister; make insight a beloved member of your family.

PROV. 7:4

Fear of the LORD is the foundation of wisdom. Knowledge of the Holy One results in good judgment.

PROV. 9:10

WE HAVE AN atheist friend whose son dated and fell in love with a Christian girl in college. Though Christians aren't supposed to marry nonbelievers, I understand why she dated him. He is considerate, handsome, brilliant, athletic, and she was dazzled by him. Besides, she undoubtedly hoped he would become a Christian.

When he didn't, she had no choice but to break up with him. But by then they were in love, and it was painful for both of them. His parents suffered to see their son hurt so deeply, and, because they didn't understand Christianity, they could not comprehend why the girl wouldn't marry their son if she loved him. They became bitter toward God and all Christians.

I wouldn't say it was *wrong* for her to date him, but sometimes things that aren't overtly wrong may not be wise.

That's why I taught my children to make decisions based on wisdom versus foolishness rather than right or wrong. When faced with a choice, they didn't ask, "Is it wrong to do this?" they asked, "Is it wise?" That simple principle helped them avoid a lot of pain growing up. Plus, because choosing wisdom is a higher standard than simply choosing right, they never had to wrestle with the bigger problems some other kids faced, like drugs and premarital sex.

What Parents Can Do

- The entire book of Proverbs talks about the merits of wisdom versus foolishness. It clearly contrasts the behavior of wise (righteous) and foolish (unrighteous) people, sometimes in the same verse. "The lips of the wise give good advice; the heart of a fool has none to give" (Prov. 15:7). Take a Bible you have not yet color-coded and, with your children, underline the verses in Proverbs that describe good (wisdom) in green (meaning go) and the verses describing wrong (foolishness) in red (indicating stop, don't do this). It may take months to finish the job, but it will be quality time that will benefit your children for the rest of their lives. If you discuss every verse as you underline, the character lessons they learn will be invaluable.

Prayer for Myself

Show me how to clearly communicate to my children the importance of acting in wisdom.

Prayer for My Children

Help them to understand the difference between wisdom and foolishness and to choose wisdom.

Study, Memorize, and Apply Scripture

> Study to shew thyself approved unto God, a workman that needeth not to be ashamed, rightly dividing the word of truth.
>
> 2 TIM. 2:15 KJV

> I have hidden your word in my heart, that I might not sin against you.
>
> PS. 119:11

I DON'T REMEMBER much about the baseball game. But I remember Pam climbing to the top of the metal bleachers to sit by me about halfway through the third inning. I don't know how many times my son got on base or if Pam's boy hit a home run that day, but I vividly remember Pam's question.

"You don't any have trouble with your kids, do you?" she asked.

"They are certainly not perfect, if that's what you mean."

"I know, but they don't get in trouble and they get good grades. Everyone knows they have character," she said. "How do you do it?"

I looked away from the game and gave her my full attention. She was wearing her nurse's uniform, which told me she must have rushed straight from work to watch Jake's game. She cared about her boys. I waited, giving her silent permission to continue. Obviously, something was bothering her.

"We've been having some trouble with the boys," she said. "I'm feeling desperate." She spent the next hour or so outlining some behavior problems and asking for my advice. I was a little surprised by the severity of the problems, since she and her husband were both well educated and likeable. They spent lots of time with their children.

The problem was, the Lord had little part in their lives.

So I explained to her how I used the Bible as my parenting manual. "I make sure my children know that every rule is based on God's Word. I tell them, 'Read your Bible. If you can show me a place where God's rules disagree with mine, my rules will change instantly.' I think sometimes they read it just to prove me wrong—that's strong incentive."

I gave one final hint. "I make the kids memorize at least one Scripture verse for each way kids misbehave. Then whenever they act up, I make them quote the applicable verse to me." We chatted for over an hour. I gave her several more examples. She seemed eager to do as I suggested, but I for some reason feared she wouldn't follow through.

She didn't.

Recently, two of Pam's now-grown sons headlined the evening news. A drug deal at Jake's apartment had gone wrong, and he was fatally shot. He died in his youngest brother's arms.

What Parents Can Do

- Giving your children time is not enough, not even if it's quality time. Stress the importance of God and his Word by daily talking about his precepts with them.
- Make sure each of your children has his or her own copy of the Bible. Spare no expense. Start with Bible story picture books and progress to children's Bibles with exciting pictures. Before they are teenagers, buy them a high-quality readable version of the entire Bible. I suggest the New Living Translation or the New International Version.

- Make it a habit to read at least one chapter in the Bible every day. If your children see you reading your Bible, they will be more likely to want to read their Bibles.
- Assign verses for your children to memorize—one a week is good when they are little. Some two-year-olds can memorize short verses such as "God is love." Search the Bible for verses that stand out to you, or start with those you find in this book.
- I made memorizing easier for my children by writing short songs to make the chore easier. I would simply choose a verse, add a tune to it, and we'd all sing the verses when we drove to the grocery store or went on vacation. I sang the songs into a tape recorder as I wrote so I wouldn't forget the tunes.

Prayer for Myself

Thank you for allowing me to live in a free society where I have unlimited access to your Word. Don't let me ever take that for granted, but prompt me to spend time reading and memorizing Scripture.

Prayer for My Children

Help them want to study and memorize your Word. Guide them to understand there will come a time when knowing your words will comfort and guide them through difficult circumstances.

Offer Biblical Advice

My son, pay attention to my wisdom; listen carefully to my wise counsel.

PROV. 5:1

Gentle words are a tree of life; a deceitful tongue crushes the spirit.

PROV. 15:4

Death and life are in the power of the tongue.

PROV. 18:21 ESV

DAREN'S MOTHER believed in Jesus, but focused more on common sense than Bible stories and precepts. Every morning Daren could expect the newspaper, opened to the advice column, to be propped up beside his breakfast plate. Growing up, he formulated many of his ideas about right and wrong from Dear Abby and radio show hosts.

As an adult, Daren continued the habits formed during his youth; he read the newspaper and listened to radio advice programs. The problem was, though he was a believer, because the Bible wasn't his first authority he never got a firm grasp on biblical concepts, and he had difficulty sorting out the truth when media "experts" twisted God's teaching.

That caused a problem for his wife, who depended on God's Word as her final authority. She didn't want to disrespect Daren by demeaning the advice columns he read in front of the children. After all, the columns had good comments. So every time the radio or newspaper gave advice, she made sure the family dissected what the "experts" had said. Did the radio agree with the Bible? Where had the newspaper columns disagreed with it? Had a slight twist changed everything? How?

By the time their children reached their teen years, they knew how to analyze and discern truth in anything. And in the process, Daren also learned a lot about right and wrong.

What Parents Can Do

- If you don't know an answer, admit it. Tell your kids you'll check to see what the Bible says, and you'll ask other people who have wisdom.
- Encourage your children to build relationships with older people who know the Lord and what the Bible has to say. There will come a time when they won't want to listen to you, but if they have already established relationships with other adults, they may still seek them out.
- Seek advice from books, CDs, and tapes while making it clear to your children that the Bible is your final authority. I used to make any teen who visited our house sit down and watch Dr. Dobson's video *Sex, Lies & The Truth*. My kids rolled their eyes and joked about how embarrassing it was, but I don't think they really minded.

Prayer for Myself

Make the words that come from my mouth offer life and not death to my children. I need your help to give them godly, biblical advice.

Prayer for My Children

Open their hearts to hear what your Word has to say to them.

Understand the Code . . .

No Other Gods

> You must not have any other god but me.
>
> EXOD. 20:3

> Jesus replied, 'You must love the LORD your God with all your heart, all your soul, and all your mind.' This is the first and greatest commandment."
>
> MATT. 22:37, 38

IN ADDITION to authoring books for adults, I write and illustrate children's books. So a person might expect schools to welcome me as a speaker, especially if I am willing to give my whole morning at no cost just so I can talk to the kids. Not in Oregon.

I recently took one of my brochures to a public elementary school near my home. The woman in the office was friendly until she learned I write *Christian* books. As soon as she found out, her whole demeanor changed. She slid the brochure across the counter with two fingers as though it were contaminated with anthrax.

"Wouldn't you like to keep it?" I asked, keeping my hands at my sides.

"No." She made no attempt at civility as she picked up the brochure and thrust it toward me. "Religion isn't allowed in our schools." I felt as though I'd tried to slip a gun into the school.

"Oh?" I promise I said it nicely. "When my kids attended middle school a mile from here, teachers took the seventh graders to the mosque."

She looked momentarily surprised, then shrugged. "Well, we do multicultural things." She turned on her heel and marched off.

Since a large percentage of the people in our nation call themselves Christian, I used to think worshipping other gods was not really a threat to our children. I've changed my mind. Under the guise of tolerance, political correctness, and multiculturalism, other gods (which are actually demons, see 1 Cor. 10:20) are worming their way into our culture and our schools. After my daughter visited the mosque with her classmates, the Muslims began sending literature to all the students and parents at our school.

More and more people in our society are being drawn into worshipping false gods. I asked the lady who does my nails if she actually prayed to the statue of Buddha displayed prominently in her shop. She said yes. I watched participants of a *Survivor* show become terrified of a storm after sacrificing a chicken to a local god. They believed the god sent the storm because they ate his chicken.

Many churches lump the worship of Jesus with worship of other gods during their services. But Buddha and Mohammed are not alternate paths to God. They are false gods, and the basis of those religions differs vastly from the precepts found in the Bible. God tells us over and over he is the *only* God. He can do anything he wants. And one thing he refuses to do is accept being worshipped along with other gods. Would you like it if your spouse brought other people home to your marriage bed? That's how God feels. You belong to him. He is "a jealous God who will not tolerate your affection for any other gods" (Exod. 20:5).

Your children need to understand that very clearly.

What Parents Can Do

- Teach your children there is only one God. The rest are false gods, God's enemies.
- If possible, purchase and read Josh McDowell's *Evidence That Demands a Verdict.*

- Volunteer at your child's school so you can keep a close eye on what is happening. Treat the teachers and staff with consideration. If you disagree with something (meaning you find it morally wrong), approach with kindness, but stick to your guns.
- Recognize multiculturalism in the schools and stand against it when it presents false religions in a positive light.
- Since your children have to live in this society, you can't completely isolate them. If you keep too tight a rein, they may feel deprived and rebel. I allowed my daughter to tour the mosque (though I did occasionally keep my children from other school activities), but we prayed for protection for her mind. We thoroughly discussed the trip before and after she went. I told her the mosque was simply a building that housed a false religion and it couldn't hurt her. While there, the Muslim in charge told the students a little about Islam's view of women. My daughter was incensed. God not only protected her mind, he revealed truth. (And by the time the next year rolled around, my complaints to the school put a stop to the mosque visits).

Prayer for Myself

Make me articulate as I speak to my children about you. Help me take every opportunity to remind them you are the only God. Give me tenacity to keep monitoring the influences in their lives.

Prayer for My Children

Grant them a strong belief in you as the only true God. Don't let them be misled by friends or teachers or the media. Give them the wisdom to recognize and accept truth.

Understand the Code . . .

No Idols

> You shall not make for yourself an idol in the form of anything in heaven above or on the earth beneath or in the waters below.
>
> EXOD. 20:4 NIV

IDOLS MADE from wood, silver, and gold may not abound in Western society, but they do exist. Voodoo dolls, African masks, totem poles, and statues of Buddha may be considered little more than decorations today by most people, but they all had spiritual beginnings. People placed them ahead of God when they needed help. That is called worship.

So if people don't worship idols made by hands, has the problem of idol worship disappeared? Since Satan never gives up but simply changes tactics, individuals do still struggle with idols. People set up idols in their hearts.

They place spouses or children ahead of God. They trust jobs to provide rather than trusting God. Teenagers reach toward the stage with tears streaming down their cheeks when their favorite band performs. Professional athletes are actually called sports "idols." A dead rabbit's foot is supposed to bring luck when, of course, only God is able to help or protect.

Idol worship is not as easy to identify as it once was, but it hasn't disappeared. Anything that matters more than God in our day-to-day lives, anything we trust in lieu of God, anything that comes between us and God, is an idol we've set up in our hearts.

What Parents Can Do

- Teach your children about the idols found throughout the Bible, and make sure they understand that worshipping them is sin.
- Examine your heart and ask the Holy Spirit to reveal any idols hidden there. (Hint: Looking at how you spend your time and money may help you identify idols in your heart.)
- Help your children look inside their own hearts and be on guard against the sin of idol worship.

Prayer for Myself

Cleanse my heart of anything that is more important to me than you.

Prayer for My Children

Help them recognize the idols they've set up in their hearts, and call them to make you the only God in their lives by placing you first.

Understand the Code . . .

Speak God's Name Respectfully

Do not bring shame on my holy name, for I will display my holiness among the people of Israel.

LEV. 22:32

They blaspheme you; your enemies misuse your name.

PS. 139:20

You must not misuse the name of the LORD your God. The LORD will not let you go unpunished if you misuse his name.

EXOD. 20:7

I CRINGE WHEN I hear someone on television casually exclaim, "Oh, my god!" because that person is treating God's holy name as common and ordinary. When I hear someone shout, "Hallelujah!" in lieu of cheering, "Yea!" when a favorite team scores, I can't help but remember that "Hallelujah" means "Praise Yahweh."

The book of Amos suggests that when those who identify themselves by God's name do unholy things, they cause his name to be profaned (see Amos 2:7). Psalm 139:20 says those who misuse God's name are his enemies.

God's name is not common. The name of Jesus is so powerful the apostles spoke it when commanding demons to leave, and the demons obeyed (see Acts 16:18). The apostles used Jesus' name to heal (see Acts 3:6–8). If a child of God asks anything in

Jesus' name it is *done* (see John 14:14). Jesus' name is the only name with the power to rescue individuals from hell (see Acts 4:12). God's name is so magnificent it causes his glory to tower over the earth as well as heaven, the place to which angels as well as unholy spiritual beings have access (see Ps. 148:13). No one has the right to profane his name by using it in a vile or offhanded manner.

It is important to teach our children to cherish Jesus' name and walk in a worthy manner so that God's name will be honored.

What Parents Can Do

- Any time your children profane God's name by swearing or using it thoughtlessly, guide them to do CPR: Confess, Pray, Repent. (*Repent* means change.) God will forgive them.
- If they swear again, you can know they aren't repenting (no matter what they claim), and you need to set up a consequence. Make it unpleasant enough they will want to avoid it. Be consistent. Do not allow them to misuse God's name.
- Teach your children the importance of using God's name reverently.
- Explain how powerful Jesus' name is.
- Inspire your children to act in ways worthy of God's name so they will not profane it with their actions.
- Warn them that if they misuse God's name, God will eventually punish them (see Exod. 20:7).

Prayer for Myself

Fill me with reverence for and awe of your holy name, and help me communicate that deep respect to my children.

Prayer for My Children

Teach them to revere and honor your name.

Understand the Code . . .

Observe the Sabbath

On the seventh day God had finished his work of creation, so he rested from all his work.

GEN. 2:2

Remember to observe the Sabbath day by keeping it holy. You have six days each week for your ordinary work, but the seventh day is a Sabbath day of rest dedicated to the LORD your God.

EXOD. 20:8–10

You have six days each week for your ordinary work, but on the seventh day you must stop working.

EXOD. 23:12

IF FAMILY or friends who claim to love us forget our birthday, we feel a little neglected, don't we? We want cards, presents, cakes, and singing. We expect family to stop everything and celebrate the day of our birth, or at least honor us by mentioning it . . . because it's *our* day. The people who truly care about us *will* honor us by remembering our day.

Because we understand how we feel about birthdays, we're careful not to forget our children's birthdays. We know celebrating their day is one way to show how much we love them; conversely, we are aware they will feel unloved if we fail to honor their day.

Long ago, God claimed the seventh day of the week as his day and commanded the Israelites to respect him by observing it. Today, most Christians honor him by resting on the first day of the week, but the principle is the same. *Strong's Concordance* says the words *rest* and *rested* from the verses quoted above could just as easily be translated "celebrate" (number 7673).

This shouldn't come as a big surprise. God worked hard for six days and loved everything he created. Why wouldn't he celebrate the birth of the earth on the seventh day? *Of course* he wants us to remember that momentous event—it's his day! How will he feel if we disregard it?

What Parents Can Do

- People of godly character show appreciation, respect, and love for God when they honor the Sabbath. Set aside Sunday as a holy day. Teach your children that honoring the Sabbath is a command, not an option.
- Jesus went to synagogue and healed people on the Sabbath. I attend church and do no work on Sundays. My parents took long naps after Sunday morning service. How you and your children observe the Sabbath is between you and God; just make certain you honor the Lord by treating the Sabbath differently from any other day of the week.

Prayer for Myself

Thank you for creating the Sabbath as a day of rest, when my mind and body can be restored. Remind me to honor you by remembering it.

Prayer for My Children

Help my children understand that the Sabbath is holy, and give them a deep desire to honor it.

Understand the Code . . .

Honor Your Parents

> Honor your father and mother. Then you will live a long, full life in the land the LORD your God is giving you.
>
> EXOD. 20:12

> This is the first commandment with a promise: If you honor your father and mother, "things will go well for you, and you will have a long life on the earth."
>
> EPH. 6:2, 3

> If you insult your father or mother, your light will be snuffed out in total darkness.
>
> PROV. 20:20

SIX-YEAR-OLD Emmy asked her aunt, her grandma, and her two brothers if they would help her assemble a puzzle. They could take turns putting in pieces, she said. They all agreed, and Emmy spread the puzzle across the kitchen table. But when her brother reached over to take the first turn, Emmy stopped him. "No! Grandma first! We're going by old age." Emmy's mother had taught her to respect her elders, and giving Grandma the first turn was a good start.

God wants you to train your children to respect others, but it is especially important for you to teach them to honor you. Not because you deserve it; you may or may not. Teach them to treat you with respect because God commands it, and they will be punished if they don't. Insisting that they honor you is one of the best ways to ensure a good, long life for them.

What Parents Can Do

- Your children will learn to respect their parents by the way you treat your spouse. So treat him or her with the utmost respect, even when you're angry. Never talk negatively about your spouse to your children. Keep problems between the two of you.
- Act respectfully toward your children.
- Teach them the "honor" commandment and the promises associated with it (see verses above).
- You can't control your children's thoughts, but you can make them *behave* respectfully. When they are young, never let them hit you or say they hate you.
- Teach them how to disagree or raise difficulties without being disrespectful.
- At any age, refusing to obey shows a lack of respect. Insist on obedience.
- When the teen years arrive and kids get impertinent, resist the temptation to let that behavior slide. Call them back to respectful behavior because of the promise and the warning attached to it.
- If they bad-mouth teachers or other authority figures, put an immediate stop to it. (That doesn't mean you refuse to listen when they are having difficulty with those people. You listen intently and take action if help is needed.)

Prayer for Myself

Help me be the kind of person who deserves honor from my children. Don't let me become so accustomed to misbehavior that I barely notice when my kids are disrespectful. Keep me diligent to command respect from them.

Prayer for My Children

Make them grow into people of respect. Teach them to honor and respect me, and give us a loving relationship that extends throughout our lives.

Understand the Code . . .

Do Not Murder

You must not murder.

EXOD. 20:13

[Jesus said,] "You have heard that our ancestors were told, 'You must not murder. If you commit murder, you are subject to judgment.' But I say, if you are even angry with someone, you are subject to judgment!"

MATT. 5:21, 22

MURDER MEANS taking the life of another person. It's wrong. God expects parents to make that clear to their kids. Kids also need to know that our laws punish anyone who kills another human. Proverbs 1:10–16 offers the best way to avoid the temptation in the first place: Stay away from evil companions.

But Jesus took the law about murder a giant step further when he suggested murder doesn't stop with the actual taking of physical life. Dr. Art Mathias explained it in his book *Biblical Foundations of Freedom*:

"God's Word teaches how we can murder someone with our words. Murder starts in the heart, because the ultimate level of the spirit of bitterness is the elimination of someone's personhood.

"Murderous hate-filled speech . . . kills a person's own spirit. Whether it is the person who is doing the screaming and his speech crucifies his own sense of decency, or a person who receives a verbal attack . . . the end result is the death of a godly, peaceful spirit."

What Parents Can Do

- If you are an angry person, your children will learn that behavior. That's why you need to rid yourself of that destructive emotion.
- Anger always masks hurt (we are not talking about righteous anger) and is an ungodly response to wounding. To rid yourself of anger you need to:
    - Ask the Holy Spirit to reveal the source of wounding to you;
    - Repent of your wrong response to the hurt; and
    - Break free by genuinely forgiving and releasing those who hurt you.
- If your children are angry, talk to them to try to help them understand their underlying pain.
- If you need to apologize to them, do it.
- Teach your children how to forgive (see the section on forgiveness in chapter 6).
- If their hurt is so deep you don't know how to handle it, seek help from a pastor or professional counselor.

Prayer for Myself

Reveal any hurt in my life that causes anger to simmer in my heart, and help me forgive and release it to you.

Prayer for My Children

Protect my children from deep, lasting hurts that would turn them into angry people.

Understand the Code . . .

Do Not Commit Adultery

You must not commit adultery.

EXOD. 20:14

[Jesus said,] "You have heard the commandment that says, 'You must not commit adultery.' But I say, anyone who even looks at a woman with lust has already committed adultery with her in his heart.

MATT. 5:27, 28

The mouth of an immoral woman is a dangerous trap; those who make the LORD angry will fall into it.

PROV. 22:14

WE HESITATE to explain adultery to young children because we think of it in sexual terms, but adultery goes much deeper than simple sexual infidelity. Adultery is the opposite of faithfulness. Parents can model faithfulness with their actions from the time children are babies.

Determine to stay faithful to your spouse no matter what. Children can feel commitment; it gives them security.

Don't lust after another person in your mind; Jesus calls that adultery.

Refuse to look at pornography, even "soft" porn. That's lusting, which is adultery.

Never flirt. That shows anyone who sees it, including your children, that you have weak character.

Let your children observe you treating your spouse with respect and love. That will allow them to see faithfulness in action.

Don't compare your spouse with any other person. Not in your thoughts and certainly not in words your children might hear. Accept your spouse's flaws, and be grateful for the husband or wife God has given you. If you find yourself becoming discontent, ask God to let you appreciate your spouse through his eyes of love.

The final verse above indicates that people who fall into adultery are already under God's wrath because of disobedience. Therefore, to lessen the likelihood of adultery, obey the Lord and demonstrate sterling character in all your thoughts and actions. Children will emulate you and be less tempted to fall into adultery themselves later in life.

What Parents Can Do

- It is your responsibility to teach your children about sex. There are several good books on the subject, and I suggest you buy or borrow one and start teaching them before they learn it from someone else.
- As you explain sex to your children, make sure they understand God intended the sexual act to take place only between married people. As early as you feel it is appropriate, put the name *adultery* or *fornication* to sex outside of marriage.
- Explain that adultery breaks up families and hurts everyone involved.
- As children grow older, explain Jesus' statements about lustful thinking as well as the concepts in the body of this segment.
- Warn them against pornography and the dangers of watching television programs or movies with sexual content.

Prayer for Myself

Help me stay faithful even in my thoughts so I can be a worthy example for my children.

Prayer for My Children

Protect them from adultery. Don't let them be harmed by it in any way as children; keep them from becoming victims or perpetrators of it when they are grown. Protect their future spouses by keeping their parents from adultery.

Understand the Code . . .

Do Not Steal

Were they caught in the company of thieves that you should despise them as you do?

JER. 48:27

They must confess their sin and make full restitution for what they have done, adding an additional 20 percent and returning it to the person who was wronged.

NUM. 5:7

FEW PEOPLE admire thieves; some thieves even despise themselves. If a person of character steals, it brings instant guilt, and the shame remains until he or she confesses and makes amends.

In fourth grade, I found a pair of shoes I loved. I was a quarter short of the total price, but the clerk accepted the money I had and told me to take the shoes home and bring the remaining twenty-five cents another time. I said I would, but I didn't. Out of pure laziness, I put off making the mile-and-a-half trek back to the store to pay my debt. Time passed and the store went out of business. Then I couldn't pay my debt. It bothered me for years because I knew I'd stolen that quarter as surely as if I'd snatched it out of the register.

My theft was a sin of omission; stealing doesn't always involve overtly taking material possessions.

Graffiti costs businesses time and cleanup money.

Wasted time at work costs employers.

Money "borrowed" from friends cheats them.

Pirated movies and songs cost companies and individual actors and musicians millions.

Unpaid rent robs landlords.

Credit card debt that never gets paid raises prices for everyone.

The list could go on and on; parents need to teach their children how those things are theft.

People of character will always feel guilty if they steal . . . and they should. Guilt is God's way of letting us know we've done wrong and need to do CPR: Confess, Pray, Repent. Since I couldn't make amends to the shoe store I stole from, I confessed to God and paid that money plus more to my church. I felt so much better.

What Parents Can Do

- It's almost guaranteed your children will steal when they're young, because children don't understand that taking what ever they want is wrong until an adult tells them. I remember one of my kids slipping a piece of candy from a store shelf. I made him face the store clerk, confess his crime to her, and return the merchandise.
- Feeling guilt when they steal is a sign of character in your children. Rejoice when you see it. Don't do anything to alleviate guilt until they've done CPR, because that guilt is from God and intended to drive them to repentance.
- As soon as they have expressed sorrow and repented, remind them that you forgive and God forgives, and the shame and guilt doesn't have to last more than an instant. It should be gone the moment they repent.
- With your children, make a list of ways a person can steal and excuse the behavior. Start with the things I mentioned and add to the list. Discuss each item with your children so that any situation they may face in the future will already be thought out, and they will know what to do when the time comes.

- Using the list, do an inventory of ways you or your children may have inadvertently broken God's commandment on stealing. Confess to each other and the people who were wronged. (Be careful not to burden your children with things about you they don't need to know.) Then enjoy the feeling of freedom that comes when the guilt lifts.

Prayer for Myself

Holy Spirit, reveal to me any ways I have stolen and not even realized it. Give me the courage to confess and make amends.

Prayer for My Children

Make them people of honor who will not steal. Give them friends who have those same values.

Understand the Code . . .

Do Not Testify Falsely

> For you are the children of your father the devil, and you love to do the evil things he does. He was a murderer from the beginning. He has always hated the truth, because there is no truth in him. When he lies, it is consistent with his character; for he is a liar and the father of lies.
>
> JOHN 8:44

> He whose tongue is deceitful falls into trouble.
>
> PROV. 17:20 NIV

> Truthful words stand the test of time, but lies are soon exposed.
>
> PROV. 12:19

STRANGE BUT true: I am a part-time private investigator, the world's most unlikely PI, I might add. Nothing in my past or present qualifies me for the job—except my husband worked as a criminal investigator for the Internal Revenue Service for more than thirty years. After he retired, he needed occasional undercover help on some of the private cases he picked up. Since I look like anything but an investigator, he thought I'd be perfect for the job.

I disagreed; I preferred writing or illustrating or even cleaning toilets. I suspected nothing would be more tedious than stakeouts. I was right. Words cannot express the boredom that weighs down a person who sits in a car for hours with nothing to do but stare at a building. Waiting. I strongly disliked the job.

Until the day Ray sent me into a warehouse so he wouldn't be recognized, and I discovered getting information from bad guys can offer an adrenaline rush. My imagination kicked into high gear, my mouth followed, and almost without realizing what I was doing, I concocted a dazzling story that charmed the suspect and extracted the precise information we needed. Wow! It was exciting. Except . . .

I had lied. It didn't matter that my intent was to help the victim of a crime.

I had lied.

I couldn't believe how easy it had been for me to slip into behavior that grieved the Holy Spirit. Worse, I had found it exciting. I repented immediately and promised the Lord I would never lie again, not even if my motives seemed good to me at the time.

And I haven't. A few weeks later, while telling nothing but the truth, I played a major role in gathering enough information to throw an embezzler into jail and retrieve two hundred thousand dollars stolen from the victim. The idea that I needed to be less than honest to do my job was a lie directly from the devil.

What Parents Can Do

- Since lying rubs off on kids, determine that you will never lie. If you twist the truth even a little, ask the Lord to forgive and change you. If your children heard, make sure you confess your sin to them. Then let them see you change.
- If you catch your child in a lie, deal with it right away:
    - Talk about why God says lying is wrong.
    - Lead your child to pray for forgiveness.
    - Role-play how he or she might have handled the situation differently.
    - Make sure you let your child know God always forgives and loves him or her.

- Assure your child of your love.
- Using John 8:44 above, explain to your child that anyone who lies is following Satan, not Jesus.
- If they continue to lie, set up consequences and follow through.

Prayer for Myself

Jesus, I know all lies come from Satan, and I want nothing to do with him. I determine to always be honest because I know truth comes from you and pleases you.

Prayer for My Children

Help them treasure truth and shun lies.

Understand the Code . . .

Do Not Covet

> You must not covet your neighbor's house. You must not covet your neighbor's wife, male or female servant, ox or donkey, or anything else that belongs to your neighbor.
>
> EXOD. 20:17

COVETING STARTS early. One of the first words out of baby's mouth is "Mine!" It doesn't matter if the toy actually belongs to her; she is determined it will be hers. When my sister's four-year-old grandson, Erik, visited a luxurious house with beautiful carpets and a winding staircase he asked, "When do we get to live here?"

The Ten Commandments warn not to covet material possessions, and parents need to teach their children not to desire things that belong to someone else. But coveting isn't limited to material possessions.

When my children were young, the two older both claimed the same best friend: Paul. He lived in the house next door, and the three spent long summer days together building cities in the oversized sandbox behind our house. My kids invited Paul to their birthday parties, and he invited them to his—until the year Ty entered third grade.

That year, Paul invited Tori and several of his school chums to his party, but not Ty. My son was crushed, of course, but he didn't hold a grudge. When Tori crossed her arms and refused to go where her older brother wasn't welcome, Ty persuaded her to change her mind. "It's OK, Tor. You can tell me all about it when you get home." He asked her not to be mad at Paul.

She cried in my arms before getting dressed for the party. I remember watching her walk slowly up the driveway to Paul's house. Alone. Twenty years later that memory still makes me ache for both my children.

But Ty was OK with it. When I asked how he was doing, he told me he'd already forgiven Paul, and he wanted his sister to enjoy herself. He wasn't jealous of the relationship she had with Paul; he didn't covet the good time she would have at the party.

Later that night, I heard giggles from Ty's room. Brother and sister lounged in Ty's top bunk as Tori shared the candy she'd brought home and told him everything she could remember from the party so he could enjoy it vicariously. Ty was completely happy for her.

I've never been more proud.

What Parents Can Do

- Coveting starts early and there's no magic bullet. You simply have to explain to your kids what coveting is when you see it, stress that it violates a commandment, and remind them not to do it.
- The problem is, if they catch you coveting, nothing you say will keep them from doing the same thing. So ask the Holy Spirit to help you notice when you covet, and then request the gift of being content with what you have.
- Let them help you compile a list of ways they might fall into coveting almost without realizing it. Talk about attitude changes that would help avoid it.
- Any time you see them covet anything, material or otherwise, point it out and discuss it with them.

Prayer for Myself

Teach me to be satisfied with what you've given me rather than coveting what someone else has.

Prayer for My Children

Help them learn to be content with who they are and what you've given them.

3

Frame the House with Strong Values

"You can easily judge the character of a man by how he treats those who can do nothing for him."

JOHANN WOLFGANG VON GOETHE

Set Goals . . .

Recognizing Gifts

> Every good gift and every perfect gift is from above, coming down from the Father of lights with whom there is no variation or shadow due to change.
>
> JAMES 1:17 ESV

PARENTS PACED the soccer field sidelines. If another player didn't show up soon, the team of six-year-olds would forfeit the game. My husband, the coach, couldn't bear it. With Ty in tow, Ray rushed over and squatted to speak face to face with shy, four-year-old Tori. Seeming to sense something awful about to happen, she tightened her grip on my leg.

"Your brother's team needs one more player," Ray told her. Ty circled his arm around his little sister's shoulders and leaned in close. I knew what was coming next and warned my husband with a glare that he better not suggest it.

Ray ignored me. "All you have to do is stand on the field," he told Tori. "You don't have to move or touch the ball." She shook her head so vigorously tears flew sideways.

"Don't worry, Tor. I'll help you," Ty said.

After a lot of coaxing, Tori reluctantly released my leg and allowed her brother to lead her onto the field, seconds before the whistle blew to start the game. A foot from the sidelines, with Ty's arm still around her shoulders, Tori faced me, rocking back and forth and sobbing out loud with mouth wide open. She never took her eyes off my face. Ty watched the game over his shoulder, but refused to leave his sister.

Eventually, the ball came toward them, and Ty's sense of team spirit kicked in. He shouted, "We gotta get the ball, Tor!" and took off running, pulling her along with him. For the next ten or fifteen minutes they swept the field as a unit, defending the goal hand in hand.

Right in the middle of it, something magical happened. The ball rolled close to Tori, and she booted it. I could see the thrill spread over her face as the ball soared down the field. Releasing her brother's hand, she flew after the ball, waist-length hair floating behind her and changing direction with every twist and turn of her body.

Her big brother reinforced her newfound skill by sending the ball her direction whenever he could and shouting encouragement the entire time. "Good job, Tor!" Beaming, she played the rest of the game with abandon.

Tori was born to play soccer.

Today she would tell you she's still a little shy, but I don't think you'd guess it if you met her. Realizing she was good at something gave her confidence. That attitude spread to other sports and other activities. Students voted her homecoming princess. As a senior, coaches awarded her Most Valuable Player in four sports; her good grades earned her the title of valedictorian.

The confidence she gained from finding one thing she excelled at spread to every aspect of her life.

What Parents Can Do

- I believe every child has at least one thing they can learn to do well. Become a student of your child. Keep an open mind, asking God to help you recognize your child's gift when it is revealed. What your child *likes* may be a clue to discovering hidden talents. Sometimes it takes a while to figure out, so don't give up.

- Natural gifts are often hereditary. The children of football players tend to be good athletes, and the children of pianists often possess musical ability. If that hasn't happened in your family and your child doesn't share your particular gifting, be careful not to not nurse disappointment. Even if you think you are hiding it, your child will sense it and feel like he or she has failed you. Instead, be open to the unique abilities God created in your child, and continually thank God for him or her. Don't force your child to become a carbon copy of you.
- Don't get discouraged if it takes a while to find a gift. Just keep exposing your children to new experiences until something clicks.
- Once you identify a gift, encourage its development even if it is inconvenient for you. (My pastor's wife used to drive her son several hundred miles from Oregon to Canada every weekend so he could play ice hockey.)
- As Ty did for Tori, be your child's cheerleader.

Prayer for Myself

Make me observant to recognize the abilities you have bestowed on my child. Then give me the wisdom to know how to encourage those gifts.

Prayer for My Children

Help them enjoy the gifts you've given them without puffing up with pride.

Set Goals . . .

Responsibility for Gifts

We are many parts of one body, and we all belong to each other. . . . God has given us different gifts for doing certain things well.

ROM. 12:5, 6

ALL GOOD gifts, natural as well as spiritual, come from God, and he's given at least one to every child. I don't know what others' gifts are, but I know my own gifts, and I remember a time I wanted to stop using them.

I'd been writing and illustrating for years, and no one wanted to publish anything I did. One publisher indicated they might want me to do line drawings for a youth novel; they hired someone else. An author asked me to illustrate her book but changed her mind and fired me in the middle of the project. Rejection after rejection arrived in the mail. It was too much. Who needed that kind of stress? I quit.

For a day.

Before I went to sleep that night, God helped me understand that the gifts he had given me were not for my personal gratification. While using them could give me pleasure, their purpose was to glorify him and encourage others. Even if he chose never to use my talents, I was still responsible to persist in developing them. So I stopped striving to be published and simply worked on honing my skills and deepening my relationship with him.

With my attitude change, the feelings of pressure and rejection evaporated. I wrote and painted simply because God had given me gifts, and I didn't intend to let them lie fallow. I still thought of creating as a job, but now it was labor for Jesus, a drink offering poured out to the Lord (see 2 Sam. 23:13–17).

At this very moment, though I have published several books, my files are stuffed with even more unpublished manuscripts. Four of them are fully illustrated books that will probably never be published, and it doesn't bother me a bit.

What Parents Can Do

- Remember that the reason for a particular gift may not show up till later in life—it took years for me to discover an eternal purpose in my artwork—so encourage your children to keep working to develop whatever God has given them.
- Assure your children that if they will diligently develop their talents, God will eventually use those talents for his purposes (see Prov. 22:29).
- If your children get lazy, don't allow them to give up on their gifts. Keep reminding them that though gifts may sometimes feel like a burden, they are from God and should be appreciated. (Of course you should also leave time for them to enjoy childhood.)
- Realize that any ability used to edify others is a gift. My niece, Carolyn, suffered from a debilitating disease that left her unable to eat, speak, or move, and stole her life at age twenty-seven. Yet she inspired and encouraged others with her expressive eyes and the grace with which she handled her affliction. What an amazing gift!

Prayer for Myself

Teach me how to gently urge my children to keep on enlarging their gifts so they can be used for the body of Christ.

Prayer for My Children

Keep my children diligent in developing their gifts, yet show them how to relax and enjoy friends and family.

Finding God's Will

He will be gracious if you ask for help. He will surely respond to the sound of your cries. . . . Right behind you a voice will say, "This is the way you should go," whether to the right or to the left.

ISA. 30:19, 21

And once again David asked the LORD what to do. . . . "When you hear a sound like marching feet in the tops of the poplar trees, be on the alert! That will be the signal that the LORD is moving ahead of you to strike down the Philistine army."

2 SAM. 5:23, 24

If you need wisdom, ask our generous God, and he will give it to you. He will not rebuke you for asking.

JAMES 1:5

The LORD directs the steps of the godly. He delights in every detail of their lives.

PS. 37:23

May he grant your heart's desires and make all your plans succeed.

PS. 20:4

EVEN IN childhood, David spent lots of time alone with God. Caring for his father's sheep on the hillsides surrounding Bethlehem, he played his harp and sang psalms. With no television or radio to distract him, he learned to ask for help and listen to the Lord's instructions. He did nothing without the certainty God approved the action and would go with him.

As a result, the Lord helped David do seemingly impossible things. As a boy, he grabbed lions and bears by the jaw and clubbed them to death while protecting his sheep. While still a youth, he killed the nine-foot-plus giant, Goliath, with his sling. Even after God established him as king, God always marched ahead of David, fighting his battles for him.

What Parents Can Do

- God speaks through Scripture reading, with a "still, small voice" that touches your heart, through an impression, a mental picture, godly counsel, or a peace that settles over you. If instruction is from him, it will line up with his Word. Pray for your children to develop a relationship with Jesus that will enable them to hear when he speaks. Not only will God give them direction, he will go ahead of them and give them success. They will accomplish every great thing God has planned for them.
- If your children want to know if something specific is God's will, they should:
    - Pray for wisdom and direction.
    - Ask advice from wise people who know the Scriptures.
    - Check the Scriptures; God will never lead them to do something his Word forbids.
    - Remember that what appears to be a logical solution may not be God's plan.
    - Listen to those niggling feelings that something is wrong; that vague uneasiness may be from the Lord.
    - Put out a "fleece" as Gideon did (see Judg. 6:36–40), and believe God will answer.

- Walk through open doors and assume God is opening them, while asking God to close the doors to anything out of his will.
- If they've honestly sought God's direction and still can't figure it out, they should not give up, because God is the one who fulfills the desires of the heart (see Ps. 21:2).

Prayer for Myself

Give me the faith to believe you can work out the details of my children's lives, fight every battle for them, and keep them in your will.

Prayer for My Children

Teach my children to draw close to you so you can fulfill every good thing you have planned for them.

Set Goals . . .

God's Will in Bad Times

These trials will show that your faith is genuine.

1 PET. 1:7

For God called you to do good, even if it means suffering.

1 PET. 2:21

And we know that God causes everything to work together for the good of those who love God and are called according to his purpose for them.

ROM. 8:28

PEOPLE OF character are not destroyed by trials; they come through stronger than when they go in. Rather than hardening their hearts, they learn compassion; instead of giving up, they learn to hope.

Life is difficult, and chances are you're going through something hard right now. If you aren't, you will eventually. Guaranteed. Your children will face tough times, too, and you'd prevent it if you could, but you can't. Instead, teach your children how to face bad times and come through with stronger character.

What Parents Can Do

- Teach your children why God allows tough times:
  - Bad times produce godly character if we handle them correctly; we learn from the things we go through, and we also learn by watching others suffer.

    - Tough times reveal our character and allow us to make corrections.
    - They order our priorities by helping us understand what really matters.
    - Difficulties teach us we can count on God's help . . . always, but in his time.
    - Suffering teaches compassion.
- Teach your children to view bad things from God's perspective:
    - God promises everything will work out for good, even the bad things, even the mistakes your children make. God can weave all things together to make something unique and beautiful.
    - Psalm 139 says God has a purpose for your children. Because they are "called according to his purpose for them" (Rom. 8:28), he's leading them through *all* things—even the failures. He can redeem anything and rescue anyone.
    - Your children are God's project, and projects rarely happen instantly. He is dedicated to developing their character over a lifetime. That's his job.

Prayer for Myself

Help me keep believing your Word, even when it seems illogical. When life looks bleak, help me to remember you are on the job changing things. Help me believe what you say rather than what I see.

Prayer for My Children

Teach them to see problems through your eyes and to trust they are secure in you.

Set Goals . . .

Learn to Be Blessed

Then I realized that these pleasures are from the hand of God. For who can eat or enjoy anything apart from him? God gives wisdom, knowledge, and joy to those who please him.

ECCLES. 2:24–26

He is the faithful God who keeps his covenant for a thousand generations and lavishes his unfailing love on those who love him and obey his commands. But he does not hesitate to punish and destroy those who reject him.

DEUT. 7:9, 10

If you will only obey me, you will have plenty to eat. But if you turn away and refuse to listen, you will be devoured by the sword of your enemies. I, the LORD, have spoken!

ISA. 1:19, 20

You will experience all these blessings if you obey the LORD your God.

DEUT. 28:2

If you love me, obey my commandments.

JOHN 14:15

THOUGH GOD sometimes graciously blesses people who don't deserve it, he went to great lengths to teach his children that the bad and good things that happen are not an accident. An individual's own actions determine the way God works in his or her life.

Before the Israelites crossed the Jordan River to claim their Promised Land, Moses called the community of more than two million adults and children together and recited the Lord's laws in a lengthy speech that listed every regulation. It starts in Deuteronomy 5 and continues for the next twenty-one chapters. Perhaps some in the audience would have been tempted to fidget or daydream, but Moses punctuated God's words with dire warnings about unspeakable curses that would have caused even the most immature to snap to attention.

The same day they crossed the river, Moses set up several large stones, coated them with plaster, and wrote down every single one of the laws he had recited earlier. When Moses finished the job, he reiterated that if the community wished to be blessed they would obey.

Then to add punch to the message, Moses divided the group in half, and they climbed to the tops of two hills facing each other across a deep valley. From the top of Mount Gerizim, more than a million people proclaimed they would be blessed if they obeyed the law; from the top of Mount Ebal the other million proclaimed a curse for disobedience.

Then with the entire congregation still standing at the tops of the hills, the Levites shouted the curses that would plague them if they disobeyed. After every unspeakable curse, the people responded, "Amen." They heard. They understood. They had no excuse.

It's shocking that a few years later they chose blatant disobedience and suffered every horrible curse, even eating their own children during famine. Deuteronomy 27–28 gives those details; the blessings for obedience were wonderful.

God still blesses people who obey him with willing hearts (see James 1:17). But when we choose to disobey the Bible, our lives go very, very wrong.

What Parents Can Do

- Teach your children to obey you. Insist on it. Children who obey parents at a young age have an easier time obeying the Lord later on.
- Understand that God wants to bless us.
    - Second Chronicles 16:9 says, "The eyes of the LORD search the whole earth in order to strengthen those whose hearts are fully committed to him."
    - The first sermon Jesus preached started with a list of blessed people.
- In the New Testament, Jesus took the principle of obedience a step further by saying if we love him we will keep his commands. Love is the highest motivation for obedience, and I hope it will motivate your children to obey you and the Bible.
- However, if they obey simply because they want to be blessed . . . no problem. It may be a self-centered reason, but God suggested it.
- You will see examples on the news or within your circle of friends of people whose lives are going horribly wrong. Use those times to help your children learn. By simply observing actions and without judging motivation, discuss how those individuals' disregard for God's laws is likely causing their problems.
- Find specific commands in the Bible they may have violated and talk about how disobeying those commands causes problems.
- Ask how those people might still change and be blessed by God.
- If you can't figure out the Bible's stance on a particular issue, call a wise friend or a pastor for understanding before you discuss it with your children.
- Make sure your children know not every bad thing happens because we've sinned. When Jesus' disciples thought someone

had sinned to cause blindness in a man Jesus was preparing to heal, Jesus told them no one had sinned. The man was born blind so God could be glorified (see John 9:2, 3).

Prayer for Myself

Convict me any time I get out of sync with your Word, and help me want to obey you. I long for you to bless me and my children.

Prayer for My Children

I know you want to bless my children. Teach them to walk in obedience to your commands so you can.

Character Defects

So I did as he told me and found the potter working at his wheel. But the jar he was making did not turn out as he had hoped, so he crushed it into a lump of clay again and started over.

JER. 18:3, 4

FOR THREE years, I threw pottery on a wheel and sold my creations at art shows. So I know why the potter in Jeremiah squashed the jar into a lump. It wasn't capricious, and he didn't want to destroy his work; I can guarantee it. He *had* to smash the jar because of something inherently wrong with the clay.

Every potter has high hopes for each pot he begins. But sometimes as he presses into the lump of clay and pulls upward, thinning the walls to shape the pot, things go wrong. He'll feel the bump, bump, bump of an air bubble beneath his fingertips, or he'll detect a hard lump of limestone.

He knows the clay is flawed, and he must deal with the defect. If he ignores it, the pot will gradually become misshapen and may eventually fly off the wheel. If he manages to turn out a decent-looking pot despite the flaw, the pot will likely explode during firing.

So he stops the wheel and pierces the air bubble with a needlelike tool called a "pricker," then presses out the air. Or he keeps turning the pot and uses the pricker to cut off the lip just below the hard lump, removing the flawed portion. After that, he can proceed to shape the pot.

But if the flaw is close to the base of the pot, he may not be able to salvage it, and the entire pot has to be squashed.

Because God says he's the potter and we're the clay, I think we can parallel the air bubbles and lumps in clay to our own character failings. When God perceives them in us, he corrects us in much the same way the potter deals with clay: He has to prick us, cut out the defects, and press us before he can shape us into people of godly character.

Fortunately, God not only corrects you and me, he loves our children enough to correct and shape them into people of character, too. Though that can be hard for parents to watch, we should welcome the times God chooses to discipline our kids by letting them suffer the natural consequences of their choices.

We want children of character.

What Parents Can Do

- Since the easiest way to get rid of character flaws is by reading the Bible and applying it to our lives, read your Bible daily.
- Early on, teach your children to understand and obey God's Word.
- When God disciplines you, accept it. Thank him for forming you into a person of godly character, because people of character tend to raise children with character.
- Recognize when God is disciplining your children, and don't get in his way by excusing their behavior or trying to rescue them.

Prayer for Myself

Lord, I give you permission to correct any defects in my character. I will accept your discipline even though I know it will seem unpleasant at the time. Keep me from interfering when you correct my children.

Prayer for My Children

Teach my children to learn from your Word rather than having to suffer from their mistakes.

Reject Inferior Materials . . .

Generational Sins

For you know that you ought to imitate us.

2 THESS. 3:7

I lay the sins of the parents upon their children; the entire family is affected—even children in the third and fourth generations of those who reject me. But I lavish unfailing love for a thousand generations on those who love me and obey my commands.

EXOD. 20:5, 6

EVERY MORNING the sounds of Jim Rome's sports talk show fills my home. Though I have never developed a fondness for that program, my husband loves to listen, and now my sons do, too. As a result, I've learned a lot about Rome's followers.

They refer to themselves as "clones," and they act like clones. They think like Rome. They speak like Rome. Every caller articulates his speech with the same distinctive inflection as the host. They end calls with an abrupt "Out!" rather than the customary "Goodbye." They may not be aware of the extent to which they have absorbed Rome's ideas and mannerisms, but they've sucked him up like a straw sucks up cola. Sometimes I wonder if it surprises Rome to find so many fans acting and sounding identical to him.

And that is the perfect picture of parents and children. Just as we leave invisible fingerprints on everything we touch, our character—or lack of character—imprints the spirits of our children. We teach values, attitudes, and ways of behaving whether we realize it or not. Our children pick them up whether they want to or not and even when they determine not to. Have you been surprised to see yourself in your children?

What Parents Can Do

- If something in your children irritates you, ask the Lord to open your eyes to whether they inherited it from you. A flaw that is passed down family lines is known as a "generational sin." Figure out which of your problems or flaws has come down through your family. Make a list of them (there may be many), and begin praying through the list one at a time in Jesus' name, forgiving your ancestors for burdening you with those problems and asking God to forgive you for your own participation.
- If you see generational sins already ingrained in your children, pray for them to identify the sin, confess it, and repent. God can erase it from your family.

Prayer for Myself

In Jesus' name, I repent for participating with the sin of [list a generational sin] and give you permission to cleanse me of this sin and change everything in me that you and I don't want passed along to my children. I forgive my parents and ancestors for [name the generational sin]. I forgive myself of [name the sin] and release myself from its curse. Please help my children break free of [name the sin] so it cannot cause pain in their lives. Help me be a good example for my children.

Prayer for My Children

Help my children break free of the flaws they've gotten from me.

Selfish Motivation

Anyone who wants to come to him must believe that God exists and that he rewards those who sincerely seek him.

HEB. 11:6

Therefore, obey the terms of this covenant so that you will prosper in everything you do.

DEUT. 29:9

Those who hear the warnings of this curse should not congratulate themselves, thinking, "I am safe, even though I am following the desires of my own stubborn heart." This would lead to utter ruin! The LORD will never pardon such people.

DEUT. 29:19, 20

But cowards, unbelievers, the corrupt, murderers, the immoral, those who practice witchcraft, idol worshipers, and all liars—their fate is in the fiery lake of burning sulfur.

REV. 21:8

IF YOU'VE been skipping the verses at the beginning of each segment, go back and read the verses at the top of this page before you go any further.

If you read those verses every day and believed them, would they motivate you? Doesn't the first one get you a little excited about earning God's rewards? Don't you want to find out what they are? Wouldn't you like to know if you'll get them here on earth as well as in heaven? When you know that obeying God will help you prosper, you *want* to obey, don't you?

And how about the warnings in the next verses? Ignoring the Lord and experiencing some of that guaranteed ruin, plus the terror of ending up in the lake of burning fire and sulfur after death, are the two main reasons I accepted the Lord. I was selfishly motivated.

I'm sure God would prefer we do everything out of love for him and others, but he "remembers we are only dust" (Ps. 103:14). He understands how unlikely it is for humans who don't know him to submit to him out of love. So he uses two motivators flawed humans understand—fear of God and hope of reward. He got me.

If those selfish motivators work for God, don't you think it might be smart for parents to attempt a modified version?

What Parents Can Do

- Don't judge, or even care about, your children's motives. Lots of Christians will argue that unless something is done unselfishly it really doesn't count. I beg to differ. One could argue that even good deeds intended to benefit others are done because they make the doer feel good. Maybe that's why the Old Testament says, "When we display our righteous deeds, they are nothing but filthy rags" (Isa. 64:6). And yet, God is so generous he rewards us for everything.
- Teach your children to fear the consequences of refusing to obey you.
- As they grow, gradually shift "fear of parents" to "fear of God." Teach them that you won't always be around, but God will never stop watching, and they are ultimately responsible to him.
- Ask them to memorize the verses above, along with other motivational verses you locate in your Bible.
- As they mature and you demonstrate your love and teach them about God's love, work to motivate them to do things because they want to please God and help others. That's love and it is highly pleasing to God.

- Use positive reinforcement every chance you get. I'm not talking about candy and privileges, though both work and it's a good idea to use them. Praise them when they demonstrate good character. Tell them how proud you are and why. Keep reminding them that their good actions delight God.

Prayer for Myself

Thank you for accepting me even though my motives are so often selfish. Help me grow in love so love will become my motivator.

Prayer for My Children

Thank you for choosing them and promising to reward them for obeying and serving you.

Reject Inferior Materials . . .

Complaints

Do everything without complaining and arguing, so that no one can criticize you.

PHIL. 2:14, 15

I WATCHED PETITE blond Kirsten run cross-country races in college for two years before I knew she was blind. In fourth grade, a disease called Stargardt's had stolen her central sight and left her with blurry peripheral vision. But because she cheerfully practices making "eye contact" when she chats, and runs without assistance, I didn't catch on to her disability until I saw her reading three-inch-high letters on her dorm room computer.

"She's legally blind," my daughter told me. "She slides a little camera over her books and it projects words onto her computer. Contacts correct her vision enough for her to read them. She's grateful for that."

Though life has been more difficult for Kirsten than most, she doesn't whine about it. When her student teaching supervisor would not accept her into the classroom because of her blindness, Kirsten refused to nurse a grudge. At the end of the semester, after the teacher called Kirsten competent yet stubbornly refused to give her a job recommendation because of her visual disability, Kirsten treated the woman with kindness and prayed for her.

Kirsten refused to complain when her fiancé spent a year in Iraq; she spent the time praying for his safety.

When they married and he moved her to a strange city

where she knew no one, she didn't complain when she had to walk an hour each way in one-hundred-degree heat to teach because her blindness keeps her from driving.

I asked her parents how they raised such an amazing young woman; they shrugged and said they just treated her like a normal child. They never gave her any special treatment and expected as much from her as from her older sister. Of course, I happen to know Kirsten's mother is a praying woman. I think that helped.

What Parents Can Do

- Don't let your kids hear you grumbling about your circumstances or criticizing others. Maintain a cheerful outlook so they learn the right attitude from you.
- Teach your children to take difficulties to the Lord in prayer instead of complaining to friends. He'll often solve the problem and remove the reason for the complaints.
- Don't let them focus on problems. Help them see the good in everything and praise the Lord no matter what happens. They don't have to praise him for the unfortunate circumstance, but they need to remember and keep talking about how much he does for them and all the good things in their lives rather than everything that is wrong.
- Don't overreact to problems; they often turn out easier to handle than you expect. My mother has a strange philosophy of life: "Nothing is ever as good as it seems or as bad as it seems." She may be right.

Prayer for Myself

Forgive me for the times I think negatively, because that is a lack of faith. Teach me to turn to you in prayer instead of complaining.

Prayer for My Children

Change them into people who focus on good things and speak positive words.

Hot Tempers

Then Jesus entered the Temple and began to drive out the people selling animals for sacrifices.

LUKE 19:45

Be angry and do not sin; do not let the sun go down on your anger, and give no opportunity to the devil.

EPH. 4:26, 27 ESV

People with understanding control their anger; a hot temper shows great foolishness.

PROV. 14:29

A hot-tempered person starts fights; a cool-tempered person stops them.

PROV. 15:18

A fool is quick-tempered, but a wise person stays calm when insulted.

PROV. 12:16

IS IT POSSIBLE Jesus felt no anger when he strode into the temple, overturning tables and cracking a whip to drive out merchants? Some people argue that since anger is a sin and Jesus never sinned, he couldn't have been angry. Personally, I believe if Jesus managed to clear the temple without feeling anger, it may have been his greatest miracle.

Jesus was never hot-tempered; he displayed righteous anger in the temple because his emotions mirrored his Father's. God is an emotional being who created his children in his image;

humans inherited all emotions from him, even anger. That's why Ephesians says to *be* angry—without letting it become sin.

Does that mean anger is OK as long as I'm reacting to unfair treatment? Is it acceptable to be angry because:

Someone lied about me?

My husband cheated on me?

The boss praised my colleague and not me?

The football coach refused to play my son?

Unfortunately, the way others mistreat us or our children sparks much of the anger we consider "righteous," but there's nothing righteous involved. Righteous anger arises in reaction to sin and is not concerned with self.

We may be unable to stop our initial angry reaction to hurt, but God says we should not allow that feeling to build and spiral downward into resentment. If we let a grudge burn into our core, it will simmer until it eventually erupts in a hot temper.

What Parents Can Do

- Look inside your own heart. Are you a resentful person? If you notice yourself regularly reacting in anger, you are undoubtedly holding a grudge. Ask the Holy Spirit to reveal the source of the underlying pain to you, and when he does, let go of the hurt and release the person who injured you.
- There are two reasons for hot-tempered children:
    - You may have spoiled them and led them to expect too much from you and life. If that's the case, stop it immediately.
    - They may be holding resentment. Gently draw them out by encouraging them to talk about what is bothering them. Show them that even though hurt is at the base of the problem, their pain does not justify nursing resentment, because God commands us to forgive.

- Explain that keeping anger inside hurts them more than the person who made them angry and keeps them tied to that person.
- Guide them in ways to confront problems as they happen rather than stuffing bad feelings inside (see Matt. 18:15–17).
- Help them release the person who injured them by allowing God to handle the situation and by deciding that the person who offended them no longer owes them. *Know* God is just. (If someone has done something against the law, report it. Never ignore it.)
- If the offending party did a bad thing, don't diminish it. Acknowledge it and comfort your child.
- If your child is overreacting, help him or her understand the other person's viewpoint.
- If you have done something for which you need to apologize, say you are sorry.
- Teach them to pray for their enemies (see Luke 6:28).
- If you make no progress with your angry child, you may need to seek the help of a pastor or counselor.

Prayer for Myself

Help me deal with anger the way you want me to—by letting it go rather than nursing a grudge and turning into an angry, bitter person.

Prayer for My Children

Keep their hearts pure and forgiving so they won't become quick-tempered.

Quarrels

A troublemaker plants seeds of strife.

PROV. 16:28

Anyone who loves to quarrel loves sin.

PROV. 17:19

Starting a quarrel is like opening a floodgate, so stop before a dispute breaks out.

PROV. 17:14

What is causing the quarrels and fights among you? Don't they come from the evil desires at war within you?

JAMES 4:1

Why not just accept the injustice and leave it at that? Why not let yourselves be cheated?

1 COR. 6:7

But if you are always biting and devouring one another, watch out! Beware of destroying one another.

GAL. 5:15

WHEN ANDI'S elderly in-laws moved into the basement apartment of her home, she was shocked to discover they often argued for long periods at the top of their lungs. She remembers one especially loud argument where they shrieked at each other nonstop for three hours. It was unnerving. It also gave her insight into some undesirable behavior patterns she had observed in her husband.

Andi was especially concerned because she still had children in her home, and she didn't want the behavior to rub off on them. So she prayed daily for the Lord to insulate them from that sin, and spent time talking to her children about living at peace and refusing to quarrel. She gave them verses on the subject to memorize. She also talked to them about accepting their grandparents' flaws and continuing to honor them.

Her daughter later told Andi that during those months she resolved if she ever dates a boy who yells at her she will break up with him immediately. Smart decision. God used a difficult situation to develop wisdom in Andi's daughter.

What Parents Can Do

- Sometimes we get the impression wisdom comes naturally with age. It does not. We have to work at becoming more Christlike. Teach your children to determine they will not quarrel.
- Encourage them to be willing to give up their rights if necessary.
- People who are accustomed to quarreling may actually come to enjoy the high passion. Make sure your children understand that enjoying a good quarrel means they love sin (see Prov. 17:19) and are choosing what Satan wants.

Prayer for Myself

Keep me from selfishly insisting I am right when I have a disagreement with my spouse. Make me willing to listen and relinquish my rights rather than fighting for my own way.

Prayer for My Children

Guide my children to recognize quarreling as sin and become peacemakers.

Reject Inferior Materials . . .

The Urge to Quit

For every child of God defeats this evil world, and we achieve this victory through our faith.

1 JOHN 5:4

All who are victorious will inherit all these blessings, and I will be their God, and they will be my children.

REV. 21:7

WINSTON CHURCHILL stood five feet five inches tall, weighed well over two hundred pounds, and did poorly in school, yet England elected him prime minister—twice. In October 1941, when Churchill returned to speak at Harrow School, where he'd coasted along in the bottom third of his class, he closed his speech with "Never, ever, ever, ever, ever, ever, ever give in. Never give in. Never give in. Never give in." Then he sat down.

Churchill followed his own advice by refusing to quit. He fought his way to the top position in England and was given major credit for stopping Hitler's takeover of Europe. God used Churchill's tenacity to accomplish his will in World War II.

Quote Churchill's words to your children. (If you wish, you may change them to "Never give up," as many others have.) Drill that concept into their brains, because if your children don't stick to things:

They will suffer with poor self-image.

They will be emotional wrecks, wondering why they failed.

They will abort God's will and blessings for their lives.

What Parents Can Do

- When they are young, select promises from the Bible your children can memorize. (A promise is any general statement the Bible makes about something God will do. You can claim those for yourself and your children unless the Bible specifically limits them.) Later, those promises should help your kids stand firm when problems make them want to run.
- Don't let your children quit just because they don't like something. If they join a soccer team and hate the coach, unless they are being harmed in some way, insist they stay on the team, doing their best until the season ends. When they've finished the season, find another team or activity.
- Remind them God is just around the corner ready to work. So many times we quit just before a breakthrough.
- Teach them not to lose faith when things seem impossible. Instead remember God's power.
- Urge them to never surrender to evil. Never, ever, ever, ever.

Prayer for Myself

Help me become a tenacious person who refuses to quit when life gets thorny.

Prayer for My Children

Give them the patience to hang in there through difficult circumstances. Protect their hearts when problems come.

Offenses

Don't eavesdrop on others—you may hear your servant curse you. For you know how often you yourself have cursed others.

ECCLES. 7:21, 22

It is impossible but that offences will come.

LUKE 17:1 KJV

Let us therefore make every effort to do what leads to peace and to mutual edification.

ROM. 14:19 NIV

I'VE HEARD people who take offense easily called "thin-skinned." I didn't understand where the phrase came from until near the end of my father-in-law's life.

As a young man, Harold's legs were injured in a logging accident as he lopped off branches near the top of a hundred-foot fir. The top of the tree swung down and scraped off the fronts of both legs, skin and all. Those were the days before skin grafts and plastic surgery, so the doctors just stretched skin from the back of his legs around to the front and stitched him up.

Later, advancing age and illness caused the injured skin to thin even more. Near the end of his life, if a caregiver barely bumped his leg the skin would split open and leave Harold with a festering sore that refused to heal. It was heartbreaking. We were afraid to touch him, and his suffering was constant.

In a similar way, when individuals are emotionally thin-skinned, they keep friends and family at a distance. Any time others get close, small things best ignored and forgotten cause injury and leave festering wounds. Even when others don't intend to cause hurt, thin-skinned people decide the offense was deliberate.

Yet these people are often blind to their own flaws. In his book *The Bait of Satan* John Bevere wrote, "Often we judge ourselves by our intentions and judge everyone else by their actions. It is possible to intend one thing while communicating something totally different. Sometimes our true motives are cleverly hidden, even from us."

Satan would love to see your children develop thin skins.

What Parents Can Do

- If you or your children are easily offended, decide to change and help them change. Teach them to:
    - Overlook small offenses.
    - Choose to think about ways of serving others rather stewing about the way people treat them.
    - Decide to think the best of others.
    - Ask God to replace their expectations of others with unconditional love.
    - Teach your children not to judge the *motivations* of others. If a friend makes a comment or behaves in a way that hurts them, talk to the friend about it.
    - If the friend apologizes, accept the apology and let it go.
    - If the friend denies the accusation, accept the explanation at face value and forget about the incident.
    - If a little voice in your head warns you the answer isn't strictly honest, let the matter drop and pray for the Lord to reveal the truth to the person. Remember the times you've talked behind someone's back?

Prayer for Myself

Forgive me for the times I've enjoyed holding an offense. I know you don't excuse the behavior just because it is a defense mechanism. Please help me trust you to be my defender.

Prayer for My Children

Lord, I want them to be spiritually and emotionally healthy and to know how to get along well with others. They need your help to manage that, but I know you will help them.

Reject Inferior Materials . . .

Jealousy

Then I observed that most people are motivated to success because they envy their neighbors.

ECCLES. 4:4

You want what you don't have, so you scheme and kill to get it. You are jealous of what others have, but you can't get it, so you fight and wage war to take it away from them. Yet you don't have what you want because you don't ask God for it.

JAMES 4:2

Pay careful attention to your own work, for then you will get the satisfaction of a job well done, and you won't need to compare yourself to anyone else.

GAL. 6:4

I'VE NEVER seen anyone work harder than my son Ty when he was learning to throw the javelin. He practiced during spring track season, of course, but he would also go to the school by our house after football practice and throw in the cold and dark. He threw all summer; he watched tapes on throwing and searched the Web for more information. Then he shared all his throwing secrets with his little brother.

Ty eventually placed tenth at NCAA III Nationals and coached the sport in high school and college. But my proudest moment came the day he limped home on crutches during his freshman year in college to watch Tevin throw in a high school meet. After Tevin hurled a record-breaker, I watched Ty hop wildly on one foot, pumping his crutches above his head in celebration— even though Tev's throw beat all of Ty's throws up to that point.

When I asked Ty if it hurt—just a little—for Tevin to throw farther than he had, Ty looked at me incredulously. "Tevin's accomplishments don't take away from me." It hadn't entered his head to compare himself to his brother. Ty felt no jealousy; he had worked hard and was satisfied with his own achievements; he felt nothing but pride and love for his little brother.

I consider that attitude a greater accomplishment than any javelin throw.

What Parents Can Do

- Teach your children that God wrote down every day of their lives before they were born. No one can take away anything he plans to give them, and they will be very unhappy if they try to scoot another person out of the place God has assigned to that person (see Eccles. 3:14; Ps. 139:16).
- So God can place them where he wants them and allow them to do all the good works he planned for them before the beginning of time, instruct them to work hard in school and at developing skills and on deepening their relationship with him.
- Pray that God will make them content.

Prayer for Myself

Forgive me the times I've been jealous of others; make me content with my place in life.

Prayer for My Children

Thank you that you know who my children are and that you are preparing them for a wonderful future right now. Make them grateful and willing to wait on you to place them where you want them as they work hard to learn and develop.

4

Roof and Enclose to Insulate from Outside Influences

It may be hard for an egg to turn into a bird: it would be a jolly sight harder for it to learn to fly while remaining an egg. We are like eggs at present. And you cannot go on indefinitely being just an ordinary, decent egg. We must be hatched or go bad.

C. S. LEWIS

Hammer Together Life Skills . . .

Struggle against Evil

> I don't really understand myself, for I want to do what is right, but I don't do it. Instead, I do what I hate. But if I know that what I am doing is wrong, this shows that I agree that the law is good. So I am not the one doing wrong; it is sin living in me that does it.
>
> ROM. 7:15–17

MY FRIEND Ann Varnum's ten-year-old grandson is a pro-baseball-player-in-the-making, but his little sister, Cassidy, isn't always pleased about it. She gets sick of sitting hour after boring hour on the grass, watching him play. When a much-anticipated trip to the beach had to be postponed because Nicholas's all-star team refused to lose and the two couldn't leave town as long as his team needed him, Cassidy cried after every win.

Finally, reaching the breaking point, she wrote her brother a note: "Nick, I hate you. Love, Cassidy."

While Cassidy's note brings a smile, she's clearly already struggling with the same sin we all fight, yet the sin isn't Cassidy; she and the sin are separate. She was born with it inside her even though she was created in the image of God.

In his book *Biblical Foundations of Freedom*, Dr. Art Mathias wrote, "Paul was painfully honest about his own struggles with sin, but he had learned how to separate himself from it. He loved himself, but hated his sin. He recognized that his old nature or his flesh was not him. It was not part of Paul that was created before the foundations of the world in God's image. It was added by Satan, at the fall of man, when Adam sinned."

Love your children while hating their sin. Yes, that *is* possible. God will help you accomplish it.

What Parents Can Do

- Don't ever tell your children they are "bad." Sometimes parents tell misbehaving kids they are selfish, shameful, dirty, a liar who can never be trusted. Dr. Mathias wrote, "These lies result in children who believe, 'I am not loved,' 'I can never be safe,' or 'I've gotta stick up for myself.'"
- Realize that your children and the bad things they do are not one and the same. Ask God to help you see your child's sin as separate from your child because God separates the sin from the sinner. "It is sin living in me that does it" (Rom. 7:17).
- Make sure they understand they aren't bad just because they did something bad or have a flaw. They should never allow themselves to feel worthless; they have immense value to you and God.
- Since they were created in the image of God, they should love themselves.
- Never excuse naughty behavior because it was cute or you think your child couldn't help it or some other child was really to blame.
- Confront and discipline the misbehavior when it happens.
- Always keep in mind you are fighting the sin, not your child.

Prayer for Myself

Teach me to love and forgive myself, and make me victorious over the memories that make me feel unworthy. Enable me to release myself and believe I am not forever tarnished because of my past.

Prayer for My Children

Help them love themselves even as they accept responsibility for the bad things they do. Show them they are separate from their sin and you can help them win the struggle against it.

Hammer Together Life Skills . . .

Use Anger to Motivate

God is an honest judge. He is angry with the wicked every day.

PSALM 7:11

Then the Spirit of God came powerfully upon Saul, and he became very angry.

1 SAM. 11:6

He [Jesus] looked around at them angrily and was deeply saddened by their hard hearts.

MARK 3:5

SO OFTEN people think of emotions as bad, but emotional makeup comes from God and can be used constructively. Even anger. God built emotions into humans to motivate them.

King Saul was a timid man hiding among baggage when Samuel came to declare him king. But when God's anger came upon the new king, it compelled him to lead an army to rescue the people of Jabesh-gilead. Without the anger, Saul wouldn't have summoned the courage to accomplish the task, and the Ammonites would have gouged out the right eye of everyone in that city.

Jesus didn't try to hide his anger at the Pharisees when they pressured him to refuse to heal a man with a deformed hand on the Sabbath; Mark wrote that it flashed from his eyes. But instead of venting at them, he allowed his unconcealed anger to confront their evil attitude. Then Jesus turned and healed the man's hand.

Have there have been times anger motivated you to solve a problem? Teach your children to use anger as a motivator.

What Parents Can Do

- For young children, it's still a good idea to teach them to count to ten before they say anything when they're mad.
- Teach your children not to pretend everything is fine when they are upset. That's called internalizing anger and can lead to bitterness, resentment, depression, and a multitude of other problems.
- Tell your children that sometimes anger can be an appropriate way to communicate. An angry tone can make another understand the seriousness of the conflict and the necessity of working to solve it. (Remember, the purpose of confrontation is to help you and the other person solve the problem.)
- Lead your children in role-playing a current problem. In an imaginary conversation, show them how to direct anger toward solving the problem, rather than at the person. Tell the offender specifically what he or she did to cause pain and how that hurtful action made your children feel. If they get off track and start attacking the offender's character, remind them the goal is to *attack the problem not the person.* Tell them to speak only about things they can observe instead of attacking the offender's motivation.
- Help your children understand it is never OK to vent. Venting is directed at others and feeds the spirit of murder in us. It hurts the object of our rage and it can also hurt us by destroying relationships.
- Teach them to fight fair by avoiding:
    - Raging ("outbursts of anger"), which the Bible condemns as evil (see Gal. 5:19–21).

- Name calling.
- Dredging up things from the past.
- Ridicule.
- Nasty words and actions.
- Embarrassing the other person.

Prayer for Myself

Help me understand that anger in itself is not a sin, and teach me to use it constructively.

Prayer for My Children

Keep them from venting or internalizing their anger. Help them learn to quiet and control themselves when they feel angry.

Learn to Confront in Love

> And though Absalom never spoke to Amnon about this, he hated Amnon deeply because of what he had done to his sister.
>
> 2 SAM. 13:22

> If another believer sins against you, go privately and point out the offense.
>
> MATT. 18:15

AFTER ONE of Tevin's track meets, I noticed his black backpack lying on the bleachers near me. I picked it up, carried it home, and stuck it in his bedroom. Three days later, I found it on the hearth in the living room. Shaking my head, I lugged it downstairs again and tossed it onto his bed.

Not until later did I discover the pack didn't belong to him. It turns out, when I took it to his room the second time, he decided it must be his sister's and flung it into her room. It didn't belong to Tori, so she took it to Ty's room. Ty had never seen it before, so he assumed it belonged to his brother and pitched it through Tevin's door.

Passing the backpack from room to room continued for two months with no communication about it between the three kids. Finally, finding the offending pack in his room again, a frustrated Tevin stomped to Tori's room and hurled it onto her bed, saying, "Keep your stuff in your own room."

"It doesn't belong to me. Mine's purple."

After Ty also denied ownership, the three opened the backpack and found the name "Bret Looney" neatly printed on several books and a notebook. We all got a good laugh out of it before returning the pack to its owner, though we did feel bad that our neglect created problems for poor Bret. Fortunately, he was able to return the replacement books he had borrowed, and no permanent harm resulted.

Problems arising from the failure to quickly confront problems when we notice them in our children can create serious complications. Dealing with a crisis when it first arises may prevent a disaster later. Read the story in 2 Samuel 13–18 about how King David's failure to confront problems with his children was partially responsible for the death of two of his sons.

What Parents Can Do

- Confront problems with your kids sooner rather than later. Learn to talk things through. The apostle Paul's rule of speaking the truth in love is always the best approach.
- When they think you've been unfair, let them express their opinions in a respectful way without fear of consequences. They should know you are always willing to listen.
- Teach your kids to address problems with others rather than holding them inside. Mistreatment at school doesn't happen as often with children who aren't afraid to speak up to a bully, because they've learned to respect themselves.
- Though this wouldn't work with bullies, a good way to talk to family members is by stating, "When you do that [or say that or treat me that way] it makes me feel . . ." Then describe the hurt you feel.
- Make them understand that attending to problems is better than simmering with anger. Still, guide them to wait until tempers have cooled so they are able to control their tongues

and not say something they'll regret later. Encourage them to pray silently, asking the Lord to calm them. As mentioned in the last section, for younger kids, suggest the age-old technique of counting to ten before they open their mouths.

Prayer for Myself

Give me the courage to confront problems promptly and with love.

Prayer for My Children

Teach them to lovingly confront so wounded relationships can be healed.

Become Mature

Solid food is for those who are mature, who through training have the skill to recognize the difference between right and wrong.

HEB. 5:14

Examine yourselves to see if your faith is genuine. Test yourselves. . . . We pray to God that you will not do what is wrong. . . . We pray that you will become mature.

2 COR. 13:5, 7, 9

I USED TO think everyone figured out right from wrong by the time they reached middle age. I was wrong. I've come to know a lot of sixty-somethings who can't distinguish between the two. Even on big issues. The line between right and wrong has blurred.

Actions society considered shameful when I was a child are acceptable now. Forty years ago only degenerates dared openly disclose they cohabited without the benefit of matrimony. Now it's a societal shrug, nearly as common as marriage. The advice Dr. Laura offers on her radio program should be simple common sense, yet it seems to astonish many listeners.

God still holds the same unwavering line and doesn't excuse us when we allow the media or peers to confuse us. Hebrews 5:14 says one must go "through training" to know the difference between right and wrong. Since that knowledge is readily available in God's Word, he holds us responsible for our own training as well as the education of our children.

What Parents Can Do

- Test yourself to make sure you are mature (see 2 Cor. 13:5). Do you recognize the difference between right and wrong? How often do you choose right?
- Immaturity in your children may be a flashing signal to let you know something isn't going quite right. If a teacher or friend accuses your child of immaturity, take careful inventory of precisely what the person means. If his or her definition of immaturity matches up with the definition in Hebrews 5:14, be grateful God has revealed a place where you can work to correct your child.
- If you notice a lack of maturity in your children, help them reach maturity by insisting they do right rather than wrong.
- Role-play situations where a right-or-wrong decision may be called for, and work through different wise ways to handle it.
- Analyze the programs your children watch on television so they won't gradually become desensitized to sex outside marriage, violence, rude behavior, and so forth. Keep discussing with them how and why those things are wrong.
- Remember that since your kids have free will, much prayer will be required to bring them to maturity.

Prayer for Myself

Holy Spirit, point out any immaturity in me. Make me willing and able to admit it, confess, and repent. Help me diligently train my children to recognize the difference between right and wrong.

Prayer for My Children

Make them understand what is right and choose it.

Hammer Together Life Skills . . .

Listen to Criticism

But correct the wise, and they will love you.

PROV. 9:8

People who accept discipline are on the pathway to life, but those who ignore correction will go astray.

PROV. 10:17

If you listen to constructive criticism, you will be at home among the wise.

PROV. 15:31

To one who listens, valid criticism is like a gold earring or other gold jewelry.

PROV. 25:12

If you ignore criticism, you will end in poverty and disgrace; if you accept correction, you will be honored.

PROV. 13:18

WHAT AN amazing advantage parents give children when they teach them to evaluate criticism honestly without taking it personally!

Still, criticism hurts. That's why the automatic response to it is self-protection, usually by disparaging the "fault-finder." But even the most unfair criticism often contains a grain of truth, and if we are willing to endure the pain and evaluate it carefully, it may help us grow.

There will be times your kids will know someone has criticized you. Let your children observe you listening without anger and honestly assessing the criticism rather than striking out. Show them how you refuse to accept unfounded criticism. Let them watch you own up to valid criticism without putting yourself down. If the rebuke has merit, let them see you determine to change. They do not need to think you are a superperson and the disapproval didn't hurt; they do need to see you go victoriously through it with God's help.

What Parents Can Do

- The criticism leveled at children by peers often comes as the result of jealousy. Help your children sort out when that is the case and refuse to own invalid criticism.
- Teach them to accept criticism without taking it personally and feeling condemned; it is difficult but possible. The most important thing for them to understand is that every single person in the world is flawed. Criticism can help them recognize their own flaws, which gives them the opportunity to work to improve.
- As children mature, if something you do bothers them, allow them to tell you about it in a kind way. They shouldn't shout or speak in a disrespectful tone or call names. If they have a point, concede and compromise if possible; try to work through the problem together. Never back down on rules that are necessary.

Prayer for Myself

Show me how to respect myself so I will naturally command respect from others. When I am criticized, help me not allow anyone to treat me abusively; instead, teach me to respond correctly to the criticism.

Prayer for My Children

Help them correctly evaluate the criticism they receive, understanding and dismissing an invalid assault, but repenting when they are wrong.

Hammer Together Life Skills . . .

Hope versus Wishing

> The thought of my suffering and homelessness is bitter beyond words. I will never forget this awful time, as I grieve over my loss. Yet I still dare to hope when I remember this: The faithful love of the LORD never ends! . . . Great is his faithfulness; his mercies begin afresh each morning. I say to myself, "The LORD is my inheritance; therefore, I will hope in him!"
>
> LAM. 3:19–24

MY TWENTY-seven-year-old single daughter called me to share some ideas about hope. During a fifteen-minute break between classes at the Christian school where she teaches physical education, she led me on a tour from Genesis to Revelation.

She talked as fast as she could, quoting verse after verse and reciting a passage from A. W. Tozer. Her insights amazed me. I tried to jot down everything she said, but captured only a little of it. I knew she'd formulated her understanding about hope from years of reading her Bible and turning to God in the midst of suffering, while trying to understand her future.

"I think I confused *wishing* with *hope*," she told me. "Wishing simply means *wanting* and doesn't involve God. If you are *wishing*—in other words, if your hope is not rooted in the Lord—when adversity comes you lose hope. It's easier to believe the bad you can see than the good you can't see yet, so you give up.

"*Hope* means waiting on God and can't be separated from *faith* in him. Job says, 'Though he slay me, yet will I trust in him' (Job 13:15 KJV). Hope can hurt."

She pointed to Proverbs 13:12 as additional proof of the pain involved in hope: "'Hope deferred makes the heart sick.' The source of the pain can be found in the very act of determining to defer hope by waiting for God to act. But if you endure, God sends blessings. The end of that verse says, 'But a dream fulfilled is a tree of life.'

"Sometimes the only way I hang on to hope is by claiming God's promises. God's words from Jeremiah have been especially helpful with that: '"For I know the plans I have for you," says the LORD. "They are plans for good and not for disaster, to give you a future and a hope"'" (Jer. 29:11).

My daughter has learned that true hope is actually faith. What is faith? "Faith is the confidence that what we hope for will actually happen; it gives us assurance about things we cannot see. Through their faith, the people in days of old earned a good reputation" (Heb. 11:1, 2).

If your children will be people of character, they need hope . . . faith.

What Parents Can Do

- Teach your children the difference between *wishing* and *hope.*
- Read through God's Word, collecting promises (statements made by God) you can apply to yourself or your children. Underline them so you can locate them easily; write them in a notebook; memorize them.
- Share them with your children every time you can—when you drive them to sporting events, at the dinner table, as you tuck them in to bed at night. Be consistent. Make talking about God's promises as common as breathing.

- Instruct your children to find their own promises in the Bible and turn to them when they feel discouraged.
- Make sure they understand that choosing to wait on God and maintain hope rather than giving up or taking things into their own hands will be difficult, but it will be well worth it in the end.

Prayer for Myself

Help me understand that hope is inexorably bound up with faith, and continually remind me it is OK if I suffer while I wait on you. Give me strong hope, and make me willing to endure for the blessings I *will* receive in your time.

Prayer for My Children

Teach my children to hope in you by trusting your promises.

Choose Good Companions

A righteous man is cautious in friendship.

PROV. 12:26 NIV

Walk with the wise and become wise; associate with fools and get in trouble.

PROV. 13:20

My child, if sinners entice you, turn your back on them!

PROV. 1:10

Bad company corrupts good character.

1 COR. 15:33

Don't befriend angry people or associate with hot-tempered people, or you will learn to be like them and endanger your soul.

PROV. 22:24, 25

Do not carouse with drunkards or feast with gluttons.

PROV. 23:20

A gossip goes around telling secrets, so don't hang around with chatterers.

PROV. 20:19

I meant that you are not to associate with anyone who claims to be a believer yet indulges in sexual sin, or is greedy, or worships idols, or is abusive, or is a drunkard, or cheats people.

1 COR. 5:11

> Don't team up with those who are unbelievers. How can righteousness be a partner with wickedness? How can light live with darkness? What harmony can there be between Christ and the devil? . . . For we are the temple of the living God. As God said: "I will live in them."
>
> 2 COR. 6:14–16

I'LL ADMIT unbelievers sometimes act sweeter and kinder and nicer than I do. I hate that. Not because I don't want them to be nice (I wish the world was crammed with considerate people), but because I wish I was more Christlike. I'm a lot better than I used to be, but I started out awfully rotten, and conforming to Christ's image is a gradual process. Nevertheless, despite my flaws God views me as just right, because he can see inside me, and I'm all lit up with the Spirit of Jesus. Jesus' Spirit is literally living inside me.

But when he looks inside those pleasing unbelievers, he sees darkness. He knows the darkness indicates they are allowing Satan to control them, even though the devil is the being who hates them and is bent on destroying them.

Despite that, God loves those people and invites them repeatedly to choose him—because he wants to prosper them. That's how kind God is. And that's also why God calls those unbelievers "fools."

Isn't it logical he would warn his children to limit friendships with them and refuse to marry people who want nothing to do with him? After all, unbelievers are picking an evil being as their spiritual father whether they realize it or not. God doesn't want their preferences to infect us.

What Parents Can Do

- Teach your children about friendships from the list of verses above. Then pray they choose wise people as friends so they will become wise.

- Tell them it is not smart to ask advice from unbelievers since all true wisdom comes from God. He offers that wisdom to anyone who asks him, but unbelievers don't usually ask.
- Warn your children to stay away from people who claim to be Christians and don't act like it.
- Tell them to be cautious about all their friendships. Since they are not to marry non-Christians, it is very unwise to date them.
- Remind them God says not to choose close relationships of any sort with:
    - Sinners and wicked people.
    - Hot-tempered people who are angry and critical.
    - Drunkards and gluttons.
    - Gossips who flatter and spread rumors.
- Don't be afraid to forbid your children to be close friends with children who consistently misbehave. Or at the very least, let those children come to your house where you can oversee the activity rather than turning your children loose in their environment.
- If any of the negative descriptions in the verses above fits you or your children, determine to change, and ask the Lord to help you forsake those ways.

Prayer for Myself

Give me wisdom and courage as I guide my children to figure out which peers would make good friends.

Prayer for My Children

Provide suitable companions for them, and help them prefer to associate with people of character. Help them make a firm decision early in life that they will not marry a non-Christian.

Opt for Purity

Run from sexual sin! No other sin so clearly affects the body as this one does. For sexual immorality is a sin against your own body. Don't you realize that your body is the temple of the Holy Spirit, who lives in you and was given to you by God? You do not belong to yourself, for God bought you with a high price. So you must honor God with your body.

1 COR. 6:18–20

How can a young person stay pure? By obeying your word.

PS. 119:9

Let there be no sexual immorality, impurity, or greed among you. Such sins have no place among God's people. Obscene stories, foolish talk, and coarse jokes—these are not for you.

EPH. 5:3, 4

If you keep yourself pure, you will be a special utensil for honorable use.

2 TIM. 2:21

DESPITE THE flurry of opinion to the contrary, it is possible for young people to stay pure till they are married. I can state that with certainty because young people who have made the purity choice spend time at our house on occasion. I could list at least twenty or thirty names. All these young people in their twenties have specific things in common:

- They are dedicated to serving Jesus and spend time in his Word.
- They made up their minds years ago to stay pure.
- They choose friends who hold similar views about purity.
- They are careful not to look at or read sexually stimulating materials.
- They don't tell impure stories or make coarse jokes.

You must believe it is possible for your children stay pure by refusing to engage in sexual activities before marriage and by remaining faithful after they marry. If you believe that, you can communicate that belief to them.

What Parents Can Do

- Obviously, this is one subject you need to pour a lot of prayer into. Start now! No matter how old your children are, pray for them to keep themselves pure.
- Explain to your children that sex is something good, but appropriate only inside marriage. There are no exceptions. State it as strongly as possible during times of bonding.
- Teach them that sex entails more than intercourse. In order to judge how far they should or should not go, have them ask themselves this question: Would I mind if my future husband or wife was doing this with someone else right now? If the answer is yes, they should not engage in the activity.
- Instruct them to go out in groups rather than alone, and focus on talking or other activities rather than physical contact.
- Don't allow them to be alone for long periods of time in a car or on a couch or in a bedroom in your home.
- If your son's girlfriend or daughter's boyfriend needs a place to stay for some reason, find another home where the person can bunk. Putting a boyfriend or girlfriend up in your home

is asking for trouble.

- Never supply birth control to your children.
- If they are already sexually active, pray for God to show them the value of secondary purity. In other words, since God will forgive them and make them new, pray for him to convince them to stop now and stay pure until they marry.
- "So now there is no condemnation for those who belong to Christ Jesus" (Rom. 8:1).

Prayer for Myself

Give me wisdom as I teach my children the facts of life and guide them to choose right companions.

Prayer for My Children

Open their eyes to understand the damage they will suffer if they choose sexual activity before marriage, and then give them the strength and courage to choose purity.

Become Influencers

I don't concern myself with matters too great or awesome for me.

PS. 131:1

Make it your goal to live a quiet life, minding your own business and working with your hands, just as we instructed you before.

1 THESS. 4:11

So I concluded there is nothing better than to be happy and enjoy ourselves as long as we can.

ECCLES. 3:12

If you are wise and understand God's ways, prove it by living an honorable life, doing good works with the humility that comes from wisdom.

JAMES 3:13

I don't just do what is best for me; I do what is best for others so that many may be saved.

1 COR. 10:33

Don't let anyone think less of you because you are young. Be an example to all believers in what you say, in the way you live, in your love, your faith, and your purity.

1 TIM. 4:12

I'M NOT fond of sermons that urge people to strive for greatness, especially when they are directed at young people. Those well-meaning teachers certainly inspire, but they also burden listeners with unrealistic expectations. Most people never achieve prominence; most of us are just ordinary.

It is my opinion God intended us to enjoy simple lives, getting pleasure from family and friends and the work he provides. I shocked a fellow author when I told her I live my life by Jeremiah 45:5, which advises Baruch, "Are you seeking great things for yourself? Don't do it!" A look of astonishment flashed across her face and she tried to argue me out of it. She couldn't; I'm contented with ordinary (though I'm careful not to confuse "ordinary" with "mediocre").

Still, everyone has influence, even children. It's inevitable. It starts at a young age, and they can't keep it from happening, because the moment they say or do anything, that action takes on a life of its own. It's a law of nature.

Maybe your son includes his younger brother in an activity that builds the little boy's confidence, or your daughter's jealousy emboldens friends to gossip about a classmate, or her smile lifts an elderly person's despair. Each of those small actions influences others.

Your children *are* influencing others. Right now. Your job is to help them understand the power they hold and inspire them to be the kind of example that will impact others for good.

What Parents Can Do

- You've heard the expression "Actions speak louder than words." It's true! When the apostle Paul listed several ways Timothy could be an example for others, every one involved an excellent choice followed by an action (see verses above). Impress upon your children that to be good examples they must *act* in righteous ways.
- Play the game my daughter uses with her students to prove it is easier to lead with actions than with mere words: Draw two triangles on a sheet of paper without letting your children see

what you're drawing. Give each of your children their own sheet of paper, and try to get them to duplicate your drawing. Describe how and where to draw the triangles using only words. It will take several minutes, you may get frustrated trying to explain it, and the drawings may or may not look like yours when finished. Try again with new sheets of paper. Only this time let your children watch you draw. Then ask them to reproduce your drawing on their own paper. They will whip it out in seconds, and it will probably look more like yours than the first drawing did.

- Obviously some people achieve prominence, and your children may be destined for that. Even so, there is no reason for them to strive for fame because, if they live pure lives dedicated to God, he will use them in whatever capacity he chooses. If he wants them to be famous, they will be. If he doesn't choose that for them, struggling to obtain it will lead to disaster. Proverbs 16:9 says, "We can make our plans, but the LORD determines our steps." Teach them to be content wherever God leads. One can determine to achieve fame, compromise anything to get it, and possibly achieve it, but that's a destructive path that leads to unhappiness.

Prayer for Myself

Keep me from wanting something different for myself and my children than you choose for us to have. Make me continually grateful for everything you give us.

Prayer for My Children

Teach them how you value ordinary people. Show them the influence you are giving them. Help them choose to walk worthy so they will impact others for good.

Hammer Together Life Skills . . .

Endure

Until the time came to fulfill his dreams, the LORD tested Joseph's character.

PS. 105:19

I will bring that group through the fire and make them pure. I will refine them like silver and purify them like gold.

ZECH. 13:9

I am willing to endure anything if it will bring salvation and eternal glory in Christ Jesus to those God has chosen.

2 TIM. 2:10

I have set my face like a stone, determined to do his will.

ISA. 50:7

THERE'S A rather unpleasant pattern in the Bible. It seems every time God intends to do something great, he allows Satan to test people so severely they feel they can't possibly endure it.

Joseph's own brothers wanted to kill him but sold him into slavery instead. Once life started to improve, he landed in prison for years with no hope of release.

Moses spent forty years as a shepherd in the wilderness, separated from siblings and other people he loved.

Jesus fasted in the wilderness with Satan harassing him for forty days before he began his ministry. The Bible doesn't say Jesus chose it; the Holy Spirit led him there and he obeyed.

For each of those men, the urge to quit must have seemed nearly overpowering, but they endured and millions of lives were saved.

I don't think it's much different today. None of us has accomplished what those men did, and frankly, part of me is glad. Great achievement requires great testing, and I don't like testing (read that "suffering"). Before we can be victorious Jesus has to test us to purify us, and I don't know how I could bear the anguish those men endured.

Well, that's not exactly true. I know *how* to do it; I just wonder if I *could*. We only endure testing by completely trusting God and determining to do whatever he requires of us, because we know he'll help. Every difficulty, every problem, is a test of our faith. Will we believe he can get us through victoriously? Can I trust him that much? Can you? How about your children? Will you instill faith in them strong enough to enable them to endure any test?

What Parents Can Do

- Teach your children the way to endure is through *determination* and *trust.*
- Make it clear up front God never promises fame or wealth, but greatness in his eyes is assured if they endure when it seems impossible to survive.
- Keep assuring them he'll be with them through every problem, even when it seems he isn't. There will come a time they'll have to believe he's there when they don't feel it.
- Encourage them to welcome every test, because it will make them stronger and more capable of accomplishing God's plan for their lives. (I know how difficult this is. Every time I'm tested I immediately start begging the Lord to get me *out*! Still, it's good advice and kids need to hear it.)

- Teach them that the intensity of a test may indicate the level of the task ahead. My late pastor, Ron Mehl, suffered terribly: His father abandoned him at a young age, he battled leukemia for many years, pastoring was difficult, and he was tempted to quit more than once. But he endured. Long before Pastor Ron went to heaven, his forty-person congregation grew into the largest church in Oregon.

Prayer for Myself

Help me welcome difficulties and suffering instead of complaining when I'm in the midst of problems. Remind me you will use the bad times to strengthen me and make me more pleasing to you.

Prayer for My Children

Help them see their troubles through your eyes; open their minds to recognize the way you are developing them.

Release Stress

A cheerful heart is good medicine.

PROV. 17:22

Rejoice in the Lord always. I will say it again: Rejoice!

PHIL. 4:4 NIV

Don't worry about anything; instead, pray about everything. Tell God what you need, and thank him for all he has done.

PHIL. 4:6

Be still in the presence of the LORD, and wait patiently for him to act.

PS. 37:7

For I can do everything through Christ, who gives me strength.

PHIL. 4:13

But letting the Spirit control your mind leads to life and peace.

ROM. 8:6

I OPENED UP the September 24, 2006, *Parade* magazine and saw an article that could have emerged straight from the Bible. The title, "Just Relax," stood out with inch-high letters beside the name of the author, Frederic Luskin. Here are the highlights:

"*Think of good stuff*" because when you think about the beauty of nature or how grateful you are to be loved, it "sends a chemical message that life is good throughout your body." (Thousands of years earlier the Bible told us it was "good medicine" to have a cheerful heart. Plus, it tells us how to accomplish it: Rejoice, don't worry, delight in the Lord and trust him.)

Slow down. (The Bible says to be still in the presence of the Lord. Then it adds a supernatural benefit: God will act on your behalf.)

Stop telling yourself how bad things are and "change the tape" to "I can deal with this." (The Bible urges you to remember you can do all things because Christ will help you.)

"Recognize you cannot change the situation" and "make a conscious decision not to stress." (First Samuel 17:47 says it's the Lord's battle, not ours. So why does it matter if you can't do it? There's really no need to stress when you know it's God's responsibility.)

I did find one suggestion in *Parade* I couldn't locate in the Bible: "Take a deep breath or two." That's good; you go ahead and do that if it helps you.

What Parents Can Do

- Practice all the stress relievers found in the verses above. It may take a while to perfect learning to depend on the Lord to stay peaceful, but you'll improve, and your children will learn from watching you.
- Make a list of stress relievers God offers in his Word. You'll find techniques not included in the article in numerous places, but the last chapter of Philippians and the Psalms are especially helpful.
- You'll notice since Dr. Luskin didn't mention prayer, I didn't either, but prayer may be the number one thing that calms me.

Prayer for Myself

Teach me how to minimize the stress in my life by trusting you;

give me the peace of mind you promise in your Word.

Prayer for My Children

Remind them you always work for their good even when it doesn't seem like it, and you will always be there to help them. Keep them from worry; comfort them through sadness and stress.

Mutual Respect

Jesus' mother and brothers came to see him. They stood outside and sent word for him to come out and talk with them. There was a crowd sitting around Jesus, and someone said, "Your mother and your brothers are outside asking for you." Jesus replied, "Who is my mother? Who are my brothers?" Then he looked at those around him and said, "Look, these are my mother and brothers. Anyone who does God's will is my brother and sister and mother."

MARK 3:31–35

NAOMI'S HUSBAND treated her abusively, following her from room to room raging, swearing, and calling her names.

By the time her only son turned ten, she had finally figured out God didn't require her to tolerate it. So every time her husband treated her with cruelty, she faced him and stated calmly but firmly, "I do not treat you with disrespect; I will not be treated disrespectfully by you." With that she would turn and leave the room. If he followed her, she would repeat the sequence.

Gradually, over the next few years his conduct toward her improved, but their son had already learned his father's behavior. As an adult he occasionally treated his mom the way he had seen his dad behave toward her.

Lest the reader blame the father and not Naomi: They were both responsible. Her years of responding as a victim to him allowed his behavior.

Jesus always commanded respect. Though he submitted to murderers without resisting when it was time to go to the cross, he did it deliberately and for a purpose—to save people. But all through his ministry his very presence commanded respect. We see that clearly in the book of Mark when his family came to talk to him about the direction of his life, though he was a grown man able to make his own decisions. He did not allow them to disrespect him by taking control of him (see verse above).

Respect is an important ingredient of character. Children need to see parents treat one another with respect, even if they are separated or divorced, and children need to be treated with respect. That's how they learn to respect themselves.

What Parents Can Do

- Demand respect for yourself. Anyone who engages in an intimate relationship without taking on the responsibility of marriage is treating his or her partner with disrespect. If you accept such conduct, you are treating yourself with disrespect and setting up yourself and your children for a lifetime of pain. So refuse to have a sexual relationship with anyone you are not married to.
- Establish mutual respect early in your marriage. Don't allow yourself to abuse or be abused by your spouse.
- If you are in a relationship where you are disrespected, seek the advice of the Bible, pastors, and books.
- If you have allowed yourself to be treated disrespectfully when you begin to work on the situation, know that your spouse's bad behavior will escalate for a time, like a young child having temper tantrums because he's been punished.
- Continually call out to the Lord, praying for courage. Ask him for wisdom (see James 1:5).
- Be calm and treat your spouse with respect no matter how he or she behaves. Keep remembering that your children need to see respect.

- Pray for the Lord to bless your spouse and change him or her.
- Find one wise friend who can help you pray and learn to act in ways that command respect.
- When treated in hurtful ways, tell your spouse, "When you say [do] that it makes me feel [express the hurt]." If the person angrily disregards your pain, repeat Naomi's words to him or her.

Prayer for Myself

Help me treat my spouse and children with respect, even as I insist on respectful treatment for myself. Test me and show me any offensive way in me.

Prayer for My Children

Help them learn to "show no fear" and command respect. Protect them from my errors.

5

Install a Sturdy Floor

"Most people say that it is the intellect
which makes a great scientist.
They are wrong: it is character."

ALBERT EINSTEIN

Nail Down Good Stewardship . . .

Fiscal Responsibility

Don't you remember, dear brothers and sisters, how hard we worked among you? Night and day we toiled to earn a living so that we would not be a burden to any of you as we preached God's Good News to you.

1 THESS. 2:9

Then people who are not Christians will respect the way you live, and you will not need to depend on others.

1 THESS. 4:12

But if anyone does not provide for his relatives, and especially for members of his household, he has denied the faith and is worse than an unbeliever.

1 TIM. 5:8 ESV

THE BIBLE teaches balance. While God wants his children to give generously, he expects them to keep enough of the money they earn to provide for their own needs and the needs of their families.

Nowhere in the Bible does it indicate we should not own a big house or wear nice clothes. God never chided King Solomon for living in a lavish palace; God is the one who provided the means for Solomon to build it. In the same way, today God provides for us by giving us jobs and the ability to work. We should work to provide for our own needs rather than depending on someone else to support us. As a matter of fact, Paul actually says those who don't care for family members are worse than infidels.

What Parents Can Do

- Help your children avoid the trap of instant gratification by requiring them to save part of their allowance each week.
- Encourage them to save by suggesting a specific goal, like saving for a toy or a new bike. Later it's a good idea to start a college fund. They'll be eager to add to it if you give them their own bankbook and let them watch the numbers grow.
- If you can afford it, match their funds dollar for dollar.
- Over the last few years there has been a surprising change in the attitude of many young people, probably because they've been given too much. Grown children are content to work part-time or not work at all, as long as parents don't let them starve. Recognize that as a problem, and do all you can to promote a strong work ethic at an early age.
- Teach your children that no job is beneath them. The simple fact of taking pride in any job lends dignity to it.
- After their education is finished, if they can't find a job let them know their responsibility is to diligently hunt for eight hours a day, and consider the searching their job. If they do, God will provide eventually.

Prayer for Myself

Teach me the balance of giving to others while saving money for my children and my own future.

Prayer for My Children

Give them a right attitude about work and money.

Back-Door Finances

They all ate as much as they wanted, and afterward, the disciples picked up twelve baskets of leftovers!

LUKE 9:17

The earnings of the godly enhance their lives, but evil people squander their money on sin.

PROV. 10:16

Those who love money will never have enough. How meaningless to think that wealth brings true happiness!

ECCL. 5:10

Give me an eagerness for your laws rather than a love for money!

PS. 119:36

WHEN ASKED about finances, my husband advises young people, "Don't worry about the front door; just take care of the back door." What he means is, the amount of money you have coming in (the front door) isn't as important as your outgo (the back door). If your desire for "things" is out of control, you'll never have enough money.

Surprisingly, that principle applies to wealthy and poor alike. How many movie stars and sports idols earn millions and then end up with nothing? Money becomes a means for pampering themselves rather than enhancing lives. Like the too-full feeling after a large meal, indulging themselves bloats their hearts with discontent. The more they have, the more they want. They eventually fulfill the prophecy of the proverb above and squander their money on sin.

On the other hand, one can earn little and still have enough to meet needs. Our older son proved he had a firm grasp on that character principle when he lived well below the poverty level for two years while completing the course work for a master's degree in math. Though the low salary of a teaching assistant at the university qualified him to receive food stamps, he didn't even consider applying for them. Yet by the end of the two years, he had managed to save a sizeable chunk of his salary.

The solution is the same for all:

- Spend less than you earn.
- Don't squander money on things you don't need.
- Don't waste.

In Luke, Jesus showed us the importance of wasting nothing. After multiplying five loaves and two fish to feed five thousand, he instructed his disciples to gather up the leftovers. Jesus didn't waste even a scrap of what his Father provided, and we shouldn't either.

If you teach your children to work hard, refuse to waste, and view money correctly, they will be surprised to find dollars stretching further than expected.

What Parents Can Do

- Teach your children to value right things, like wisdom and relationships, rather than money.
- It is the *love* of money that is the root of all evil, not money itself. Guide them to understand that money should be used to enhance lives—theirs and others'.
- Teach your children to handle money by setting three jars on the dresser. In one put the money they will give to the Lord

(my children gave a ten-percent tithe). In a second, collect the money they plan to save from each allowance. (You help them decide on a percentage of their allowance that should be saved, and then insist they save consistently.) In the third keep the money they can spend however they wish.

- If your children use up their allowance too soon, don't bail them out. Going without something they really want a time or two will help them learn from natural consequences.

Prayer for Myself

Help me to recognize and deal with areas of waste in my life.

Prayer for My Children

Guide them to keep money in its proper placc and not fall victim to the love of money.

Nail Down Good Stewardship . . .

Generosity

Honor the LORD with your wealth and with the best part of everything you produce. Then he will fill your barns with grain, and your vats will overflow with good wine.

PROV. 3:9, 10

Remember this—a farmer who plants only a few seeds will get a small crop. But the one who plants generously will get a generous crop. You must each decide in your heart how much to give. And don't give reluctantly or in response to pressure. "For God loves a person who gives cheerfully." And God will generously provide all you need. Then you will always have everything you need and plenty left over to share with others. As the Scriptures say, "They share freely and give generously to the poor. Their good deeds will be remembered forever."

2 COR. 9:6–9

Give freely and become more wealthy; be stingy and lose everything. The generous will prosper; those who refresh others will themselves be refreshed.

PROV. 11:24, 25

IN MY twenties, I spent a summer working at a camp for underprivileged children. One day as counselors handed out treats, I noticed something I rarely saw in the affluent children I taught in public school. The very poor children at the camp shared everything the counselors gave them with friends and younger siblings. They wouldn't eat a popsicle without splitting it and sharing. They weren't given great wealth, just a few sweets and trinkets, but they gave most of it away, and their obvious joy in doing so pleased God.

Remember the widow in the New Testament who dropped only two pennies in the collection box? Jesus said she gave more than the rich people who gave great sums, because they gave only a tiny percentage of their money, while she gave everything she had (see Luke 21:1–3). In his book *Just in Case I Can't be There* Ron Mehl wrote, "Sometimes, Son, I find myself wondering if giving doesn't really *become* giving until it hurts."

God wants us to give sacrificially and to give to him by giving to the church as well as to people in need. He values the attitudes of love and compassion that underlie that act and promises to make generosity worth our while. If we are openhanded, he'll provide everything we need. Better yet, he'll reward us with great spiritual wealth.

What Parents Can Do

- Even though God rewards generosity, teach your children to be generous because they *want* to help others and serve God, not so God will reward them (see Matt. 25:40).
- Teach your children to give to the church, whether they give tithes or other gifts (see Mal. 3:8–12). I taught my children to give a ten-percent tithe, and I think they still do.
- Encourage your children to earn money to give to people in need. You might pay them for jobs around the house or help them bake brownies for a bake sale.
- Remind them generosity applies to more than money:
    - A person of character is generous with time.
    - A person of character shares food with people in need.
    - A person of character is generous with words of encouragement.
    - A person of character is hospitable.
    - A person of character generously prays for enemies.

Prayer for Myself

Help me depend on you for provision as I remember wealth can disappear in an instant. You have promised to supply our needs.

Prayer for My Children

Make their hearts overflow with generosity.

Poverty

God blesses those who are poor and realize their need for him, for the Kingdom of Heaven is theirs.

MATT. 5:3

But people who long to be rich fall into temptation and are trapped by many foolish and harmful desires that plunge them into ruin and destruction.

1 TIM. 6:9

Hasn't God chosen the poor in this world to be rich in faith?

JAMES 2:5

AS A KID, I thoroughly enjoyed poverty. So did my little sister and brother. Our pastor-father earned thirty-six dollars a week, and we lived in a six-hundred-square-foot, oil-stove-in-the-middle-of-the-living-room parsonage. A cistern of bug-filled water and a stinky outdoor toilet with old magazines for toilet paper completed our living arrangements. And I promise you we didn't mind a bit.

We learned to appreciate the little things. The whole family celebrated wildly when the congregation connected a lipstick-red hand pump from the cistern to the kitchen sink. Getting a drink without going outside was pure luxury, and we never once thought it inconvenient to strain water to remove wigglers.

It was all about Mom's attitude. She and my dad loved each other and the Lord, and she considered anything beyond that undeserved blessing. She sewed all our clothes. She planted a garden and canned. To beautify our home, she crafted large dried-weed arrangements that rivaled professionally done floral creations. She didn't protest when churches who couldn't afford a second pastor expected her to work as unpaid staff. She simply enlisted our help. Every summer we stretched dollars for the church by pouring hundreds of molds to make plaster figurines for the vacation Bible schools she always directed. And I loved every minute of it.

Because of my mother's response to our physical needs, I never felt deprived. Instead I learned creativity. When both my parents continually looked to God for provision instead of complaining, I learned trust. The understanding of what it meant to sometimes go without increased my compassion for others in need. Saving pennies and waiting for, or never getting, the material goods I wanted enhances my appreciation for everything I have today and helps me enjoy life at a deeper level.

I consider the poverty of my youth a great blessing. I wouldn't trade it for anything.

What Parents Can Do

- Instead of stewing over things you don't have, turn providing them into a game.
- Include the kids in your game by letting them help you clip coupons or decorate the house with cones you pick up in the park. When my mom treated us that way, my siblings and I ended up with feelings of accomplishment and competency.
- If you are creatively challenged, check out books from the library that show you how to make something from almost nothing.
- Almost unfortunately, our society has prospered, and most of us are rich by the rest of the world's standards. Still, I would advise you to raise your kids as though you aren't wealthy. Living in a beautiful house and driving a nice car is wonderful, but don't give your kids everything they ask for. When

they really want something, make them earn money and save for it. It will be so much sweeter when they finally get it.
- Teach them that the purpose of God-given blessings is so we can share with others (see 2 Cor. 8:13, 14).

Prayer for Myself

Teach me to be grateful for the things I have. Make me rich in faith.

Prayer for My Children

Guide my children to want the important things in life rather than material goods.

Nail Down Good Stewardship . . .

Pets

> The godly care for their animals, but the wicked are always cruel.
>
> PROV. 12:10

> Know the state of your flocks, and put your heart into caring for your herds.
>
> PROV. 27:23

I NEVER DID figure out how my three-year-old son caught and killed a half-grown chicken, but he did. He made no attempt to lie about it when I discovered the carcass buried in his sandbox. "Ty, did you do that?"

"I killed the chickie." I was in shock.

"On purpose?"

He didn't know. But since serial killers often start out torturing animals, I needed an answer. "Did you know *before* you killed the chickie that it would die? Or did it surprise you when it didn't move anymore?" I asked.

He looked confused.

Over the next three days I cried a lot and asked him many times in many different ways if he killed the chicken deliberately. I desperately wanted it to be an accident, like the way kids caress butterflies and worms to death. I never got an answer.

On the fourth day, Ty asked me a question from his car seat behind me on the way to preschool. "If I say I didn't kill the chickie on purpose, will you still be mad?"

Great. I was teaching my son to lie.

Immediately, I assured him he was forgiven, and I determined to be content with never knowing the truth, though I spent a lot of time in prayer over it. For a while I chided myself for possibly causing harm by overreacting (parenting is a guilt-ridden business, isn't it?), but in retrospect I believe it was not only OK for him to understand how upset I was that he killed a living thing, he needed to know. He never harmed another animal.

Later, after coyotes killed the remainder of our chickens, we acquired a series of cats, mice, and cows, plus a couple of dogs and a rabbit. All of them, except the beef cattle we stored in the freezer, died natural or accidental deaths. Today, Ty and I both eat chicken without guilt.

What did Ty learn from our animals?

Responsibility. He understood if he didn't feed, water, and brush them and make sure they were sheltered in cold weather, no one else would. (Of course, *you* know my husband and I would have, but don't tell Ty.)

He learned to give love and be considerate.

He learned about death and how to grieve.

What Parents Can Do

- Since love is an action, caring for pets is a great way to teach children how to love.
- Though most people in Bible times owned animals, the Bible does not command that you give your child a pet. Still, I would advise you give them an easy-to-care-for fish if you think the responsibility of a kitten or puppy is too much.
- If you get them a pet, understand you will be the one who makes sure the animal is cared for. That doesn't mean your children are not learning responsibility. It just means they are *still learning* responsibility. You're the teacher.
- Realize that animals can be a great comfort to children when troubles come.

Prayer for Myself

Show me whether I should allow my children to have pets.

Prayer for My Children

If your children have pets, use their pets to teach life lessons. Help them learn to be gentle, considerate, responsible, and loving as they care for their pets.

Build Healthy Attitudes . . .

Self-Esteem

For God loved the world so much that he gave his one and only Son, so that everyone who believes in him will not perish but have eternal life.

JOHN 3:16

I have loved you, my people, with an everlasting love. With unfailing love I have drawn you to myself.

JER. 31:3

God decided in advance to adopt us into his own family by bringing us to himself through Jesus Christ. This is what he wanted to do, and it gave him great pleasure.

EPH. 1:5

If we live, it's to honor the Lord.

ROM. 14:8

Our goal is to please him.

2 COR. 5:9

Carefully determine what pleases the Lord.

EPH. 5:10

THE STORY of Goldilocks and the Three Bears makes me think of self-esteem. The little girl with blonde curls found one of the bears' beds too hard, another too soft, and one just right. Refusing to tolerate either of the uncomfortable beds, Goldilocks searched till she found the "just right" bed, sank into it, and peacefully fell asleep.

As I see it, the bears' beds correspond to the three ways children might view themselves:

- *Too hard.* They might be too hard on themselves because they suffer from low self-esteem. It causes them pain and often manifests itself as faults that drive friends away. They ache from feelings of worthlessness and loneliness.
- *Too soft.* They choose to be too soft on themselves and compensate for an underlying lack of self-worth by deciding they are superior to others. While this arrogance may seem less painful than low self-esteem, it can hurt others and destroy relationships.
- *Just right.* They can be "just right" and simply live confidently without thinking much about themselves. Only this form of self-esteem offers peace.

But how do you help your children become confident, well-adjusted individuals with a healthy self-esteem even if you suffer from low self-esteem and your spouse is arrogant? The path is different than most parents believe.

What Parents Can Do

- Don't be critical. Stop coming down on yourself so hard (self-criticism), and appreciate yourself as a valued child of God. Then maybe you can accept your children and love them for who they are. None of us ever reaches perfection, and God loves and accepts us anyway.
- Don't try to build their sense of self with flattery or join them in exalting themselves above others. Their abilities are gifts, and they have no right to brag or feel superior. (Read how God feels about flattery in Psalm 12:3.)
- Remember that Low Self-Esteem and Arrogance are like twins who always walk around together holding hands. If you spot Arrogance, you can be sure Low Self-Esteem is right there, too, even if Arrogance doesn't know it.
- Teach them who they are:

- They are your much-loved children. Prove it by daily showing them physical and verbal affection.
- They are the much-loved children of God, and he says they have great worth. He loved them so much he decided to adopt them into his own family before they were even born. He considers them so valuable he sent his only Son to earth to die for them. If they think they are worth less than God says, they are essentially saying he is lying.
- They are children who will make mistakes without losing value in your eyes or God's eyes. Do the following to make that clear:
    - Offer them a ten-dollar bill. Then crumple it and offer it to them again. Stomp on it, pretend-spit on it, rub dirt on it. Do they still want it? (They will.) Make the point that no matter what the bill went through, it still retained its full value. In the same way, nothing can ever diminish their value in your eyes, because of who they are . . . yours. And God's. (You may wish to frame that ten-dollar bill and hang it on their wall to continually remind them of their worth.)
    - Tell them to learn what Jesus wants and live to please him alone. Then they won't have to worry about the opinions of others.

Prayer for Myself

Show me what pleases you, and teach me to live for your approval alone. Help me not to worry or allow my mistakes to fill me with a sense of worthlessness and depression.

Prayer for My Children

Give each of them a healthy self-esteem. Establish their focus on you, and make them confident without being conscious of self.

Build Healthy Attitudes . . .

Teachability

> Then he said, "I tell you the truth, unless you turn from your sins and become like little children, you will never get into the Kingdom of Heaven. So anyone who becomes as humble as this little child is the greatest in the Kingdom of Heaven."
>
> MATT. 18:3, 4

I'VE SPENT a lot of time wondering precisely what the Bible means when it says we should become like little children. Does that mean children please the Lord more than I do as an adult? What about children pleases God?

In his book *How to Stop the Pain* Dr. James B. Richards shed some light on my questions. He said children dwell almost constantly in the "alpha state" until about age ten. He explained: "In professional terms, the meditative state wherein one's heart is easily influenced is called the 'alpha state.' The alpha state is reached in times of deep prayer, meditation, or simply deep thought and study. . . . In the alpha state, the conscious mind loses its grip on the thought process, and the thoughts of the heart begin to emerge. The heart is also more vulnerable at this point."

That tells us the quality in children that so pleases the Lord is their teachable spirit, their willingness to listen and change, the way they can be easily influenced. We have a great opportunity to shape godly character in our children if we understand and continually instruct them in the ways of the Lord during those early years. They'll pay attention if we point out right and wrong while they are young.

In addition, we can teach our children how to deliberately spend time in the alpha state. By developing habits of prayer, meditation, and study they will be able to make their hearts vulnerable to God throughout their lives.

What Parents Can Do

- When they are young, let your children observe you spending quiet time with the Lord as you model daily prayer and Bible study.
- Over and over, fill their minds with words about the importance of study, meditation, and prayer. "Wash their brains" with the importance of seeking God in those ways. (Someone said if you hear something thirteen times it becomes truth, and I've heard that statement often enough I believe it.)
- Make sure they understand it takes time to develop a heart attitude that pleases the Lord.
- Caution: Several religions teach the value of meditation. The problem is, there are powerful spirits at work in our world other than God. Ephesians 6 calls them "the evil rulers and authorities of the unseen world." So teach your children never to simply open their hearts, but to make certain they are focused on the God of the Bible before they begin to meditate or pray. Then their hearts won't be influenced by wrong spirits and attitudes.

Prayer for Myself

Help me become childlike and vulnerable to you.

Prayer for My Children

While my children are in the alpha state, shape their character until they become more and more like you, Jesus.

Build Healthy Attitudes . . .

Thoughtfulness and Consideration

Let everyone see that you are considerate in all you do.

PHIL. 4:5

IN EARLY June 1976, record-breaking heat beat down on Oregon for several days in a row. Six months pregnant with my first child and teaching in a junior high with no air conditioning, I fought exhaustion.

One sweltering Friday during my last-period social studies class, my pregnant brain refused to function. I struggled to concentrate. I could barely keep my eyes open. How could I lead a discussion?

Fifteen minutes into the class, I launched into survival mode: I would do what I had to in order to get through the next half hour. "Take out your textbooks," I told the eighth graders. "We're going to take turns reading."

Though I rarely sat during class, I lumbered over to my desk and sank into my chair. I opened my teacher's edition and pretended to read along, but my eyes weren't focused on the words. I kept thinking, *I* will *stay awake. I* will *stay awake. I* will . . .

I woke up to the monotone of a male voice reading. After a minute or two, he stopped, and a female voice picked up where he left off. Other than that, and the buzz of a fly somewhere to my left, the room was silent. Carmen Bony was standing in front of the room like a teacher, textbook in hand, eyes watching everyone. As soon as she noticed I was awake, she whispered,

"Go back to sleep, Mrs. Taylor. I've got it." Several heads around the room bobbed in agreement.

Eighth graders! Why didn't some of the rowdy boys act out? Certainly they were tempted.

I give the credit to Carmen Bony. When she was young, her parents stressed the importance of being considerate, and Carmen saw her parents treat others with kindness. As a result, she felt strongly enough about it she was able to convince an entire public school class to extend mercy to an exhausted teacher.

Considerate people are often influential people.

What Parents Can Do

- Recognize that since selfishness is the natural state of humans, we must all work to overcome it. Only as we learn to put the welfare of others ahead of our own do we become considerate people.
- Treat your children with consideration, and let them see you treating others with consideration. Your children learn by watching you.
- When you read to your young children, praise the considerate characters in the book and explain why you approve of their actions. Talk about precisely what it means to be considerate.
- When young children are inconsiderate, mention it to them, and discuss how they might have been nicer.

Prayer for Myself

Help me see myself as you see me. Point out those times I am not considerate. Make me willing to change my ways and willing to apologize when necessary.

Prayer for My Children

Prick the hearts of my children when they are inconsiderate. Give them a strong desire to think of others first.

Build Healthy Attitudes . . .

Empathy

> Rejoice with them that do rejoice, and weep with them that weep.
>
> ROM. 12:15 KJV

EMPATHY IS a precious quality in children and adults alike. Unfortunately it is usually learned through painful experience. While deep hurt at an early age deadens some to the suffering of others (as is the case with most sociopaths and violent criminals), a limited level of pain is one of the best ways to teach children the quality of empathy.

My daughter tells me she developed empathy as a result of being mistreated by other girls in her third-grade classroom. Though it felt terrible at the time, today she is grateful for the experience.

However, my husband and I protected her by stepping in to limit her pain in a couple of ways. Because we lived next door to the school, we got permission for her to come home at noon any time she chose, which meant when she had a bad day she could check in with the teacher, no explanations necessary, and walk to the house to eat with me. After she finished eating and we'd hugged and talked and prayed, she'd feel comforted enough to return to school.

Also, since she played soccer with those same classmates after school, we switched her to a classic team across town, where she could interact with other girls her age who would treat her with kindness. It was inconvenient; I drove her forty-five minutes each way in rush-hour traffic for practice every day. But it was well worth the effort.

If we could have banished all Tori's pain that year we might have. Fortunately we could offer enough support to mitigate the damage. If we had done more, she would never have experienced the hurt that deepened her character by teaching her to empathize with others who are wounded.

What Parents Can Do

- Provide a safe haven for your children, but ask God to keep you out of the way when you are tempted to block the painful circumstances he intends as character development.
- Talk through every difficulty with them. As you talk, give an abundance of hugs, assure them of your love and their worth, and tell them things will get better.
- Though it sounds like an excuse, often bad treatment simply means the perpetrator is jealous of the victim, especially in the case of girls. If that is true, help your child understand it.
- Pray with them and guide them to ask God to bless their enemies. Don't worry; God will only bless people as they repent and change, so a prayer for blessing is a prayer for bullies to turn from wickedness (see Acts 3:26). As your children obey God's command to pray for enemies, they open the way for those enemies to become potential friends.
- As your children grow older, if they treat you badly don't be afraid to let them know you are human and they hurt you. Don't manipulate them; just help them understand parents are people with feelings, too.
- When your children do wrong, don't minimize what they did because you see them hurting and you can't stand to see them suffer. Agree they did wrong and it was a sin. Tell them how glad you are they told you about it. Explain they now need to

confess to God. He forgives. Even though they may still need to suffer the natural consequences, he will wipe away their guilt.

Prayer for Myself

It hurts me so much when I see my children in pain. Give me courage to let them suffer when necessary so they will learn the quality of empathy. Show me how to reassure them instead of trying to remove their pain.

Prayer for My Children

Comfort them in the midst of their pain, but use that pain to make them empathetic.

Rejoice with Others

Be happy with those who are happy.

ROM. 12:15

SOPHIA WROTE beautifully, but no publishers ever wanted anything she sent them. It broke her heart.

When she met Nancy, the published author of one book, I expected Sophia to feel a little inferior, maybe even jealous. Instead, Sophia was happy to learn Nancy had written a second book that would be published soon. Later, when the company threatened to pull Nancy's contract, Sophia cried with her friend. She committed to help Nancy improve her writing and promised to pray for her every day.

For the next five years Sophia did exactly that; she continually prayed for God to bless Nancy; she offered suggestions on all her friend's writings, and she and Nancy regularly met for brainstorming sessions. Sophia freely gave ideas to Nancy, who put them to good use in her books. Sophia never once regretted giving ideas away; she was thrilled Nancy could use them. Sophia said all ideas came from God, and he would continue to send them. Why should she hang on to them for herself?

During that five years, Nancy published nearly forty books, and Sophia was as excited as her friend every time Nancy called to say a new contract had arrived in the mail. Even though Sophia continued to write without getting published, she never felt jealous of her friend. Not once.

God later rewarded Sophia with a book contract.

What Parents Can Do

- Let your kids know God expects us to be happy for other people when good things happen to them.
- Make sure they understand that the accomplishments of someone else don't add to or diminish your children's achievements. When they see another person succeed it should inspire them to do better.

Prayer for Myself

Make me truly happy way down deep in my heart when you bless other people.

Prayer for My Children

Let my children notice my attitude of joy for others and imitate me.

Perseverance

Don't you realize that in a race everyone runs, but only one person gets the prize? So run to win! All athletes are disciplined in their training.

1 COR. 9:24, 25

For this very reason, make every effort to add to your faith goodness; and to goodness, knowledge; and to knowledge, self-control; and to self-control, perseverance, and to perseverance, godliness.

2 PET. 1:5, 6 NIV

And let us run with perseverance the race marked out for us.

HEB.12:1

I CAN'T TELL you how ready I was for that 10K race—the first since the birth of my three children. I'd been going to the Jackson Middle School track daily since a couple of weeks after my third cesarean birth, and I was *ready.* I could tell because I passed runner after runner on the track every day. Sure, I was a little slower than I'd been six years earlier, and occasionally a fit younger guy would show up and lap me a couple of times, but I was basically queen of the track. You would have been dazzled. So when my husband suggested I sign up for a 6.2-mile race, I eagerly agreed.

Thousands of athletes showed up the day of the race. They crowded against me on every side, hemming me in. I wasn't worried; as soon as the crowd thinned, I'd break free and start passing people.

The gun sounded to start the race. Gradually the runners ahead began pulling ahead of the pack surrounding me, and I sensed I would soon have space to break away and make my move.

Unfortunately, it never happened. Instead, the pack left me in their dust, and people from behind started passing. Hundreds of them streamed by until all I could see were the backs of other runners.

Eventually, with a mile or so left in the race I could see only scattered runners on the road in front of me, and I couldn't find a single one behind me. Whenever spotters up ahead caught sight of me they would cup hands around their mouths and call out, "Here comes the last runner!" I could hear the news ripple up the lines of spectators. How embarrassing! That's when I figured out no runners from the middle school track had signed up for the race.

I confess to being tempted to slither out of the race and hide, but I didn't. I persevered and finished. And to my surprise, hundreds of slower runners trailed in after I crossed the finish line! Though I didn't win, I count it a victory because I persevered.

What Parents Can Do

- Teach your children the importance of persevering. Life will get difficult. Your kids must determine before problems arise they will exercise self-control and persevere.
- Assure your kids perseverance leads to godliness (see the 2 Peter verse above).
- Tell them it's not as important to *be* the best as it is to *do* their best. The goal should be to please God. He is happy when your kids work up to their ability level, and you should be, too.

- Keep reminding them to enjoy a sense of satisfaction when they stick with something and finish it. That's not pride; God wants them to feel good about the things they do (see Gal. 6:4).
- Conversely, help them understand that sometimes it may be wise to quit. My husband and I drummed the idea of perseverance into our kids' heads so strongly that sometimes they don't understand when to quit. Once my daughter seriously considered returning to a job that had put her life in jeopardy. It took a while to convince her it was OK to quit.

Prayer for Myself

Give me the courage to persevere when things get tough.

Prayer for My Children

Help them believe perseverance is a trait to be desired. Make them people of courage.

Patience

On thee do I wait all the day.

PS. 25:5 KJV

Let all that I am wait quietly before God, for my hope is in him.

PS. 62:5

God waited patiently while Noah was building his boat.

1 PET. 3:20

But those who trust in the LORD will find new strength. They will soar high on wings like eagles. They will run and not grow weary. They will walk and not faint.

ISA. 40:31

I LOVE PSALM 25:5 because it is so stark, so honest, so . . . me. Why must I wait on the Lord all . . . day . . . long? I don't like it. When I don't get what I want and things don't go as anticipated, I expect God to change it *now*! The problem is, I rarely have any control over the situation, which forces me to wait on God, and he doesn't seem to move very fast. Even when conditions resolve temporarily, the issue invariably pops up again days or weeks or months later. And I have to deal with the same problem over and over and over. Why?

Once when I was pummeling God with that question, I found a little verse tucked into 1 Peter that explained it. The verse says *God* waited patiently on *Noah* to finish the ark. Noah had to do his part before God could send the Flood.

Noah wasn't the one waiting; God was.

Whoa! That means sometimes I only imagine I'm waiting on God when, really, he's waiting on me. He's showing kindness by refusing to give me the things I want before I've prepared properly. Other times he knows the timing isn't right, and rushing things would ruin everything.

Of course God could have sent the Flood before Noah finished the ark, but that would have wiped the earth clean. Food for thought: Do you want God to send what you're demanding before he knows you can handle it properly?

What Parents Can Do

- Your children will have lots of times to practice patience. Let them know they haven't mastered the skill until they can manage waiting with a good attitude.
- Let them know there are four ways to develop patience:
    - Circumstances will teach them.
    - The consequences of sin will teach them.
    - Jesus can teach them as they force him to discipline them.
    - They can *choose* it for themselves.
- Offer your children a few reasons to choose waiting patiently on God:
    - If he made your son the star on the basketball team when the boy wanted it so desperately, it might have become an idol to him.
    - If he gave your daughter influence while she was immature, it would lead to pride and her downfall (see 1 Tim. 3:6).
    - If he allowed your kids to marry the first person they were certain was the right one, they could end up divorced.
    - If your children refuse to study in school and neglect the hard work necessary to develop skills, they won't be able to shine for God on the job.

Prayer for Myself

Teach me to wait patiently as you show me what I need to do in the midst of problems. Give me the wisdom to know when I can do nothing but patiently wait on you, because you have all power and I have none. Help me willingly turn control over to you.

Prayer for My Children

Help them *choose* to patiently wait for you through every problem. Make them willing to wait for you to give them the desires of their hearts instead of trying to meet their own needs. I want them to avoid the problems I have faced. I know you will give them strength and wisdom as they wait on you.

Relaxed Attitude

A peaceful heart leads to a healthy body.
PROV. 14:30

IN THE car on the way to pick her brother up at Sports Fitness Camp, my seven-year-old daughter suddenly realized she had stepped in cat poo in the sandbox and had it between her toes and on one hand. In the rearview mirror, I could see her in the middle of the seat behind me with the offending hand held stiffly in a palm-up, claw-like position. I expected a loud complaint; instead she stared straight ahead and rocked stoically.

I assumed she understood we couldn't soap up and wash off the offending body parts until we arrived back home, and had decided to endure without complaining. I was impressed. That was quite an improvement in my occasionally naughty little girl.

As soon as Ty opened the car door and buckled into the passenger seat, Tori explained her predicament to him. He sympathized with her, and then we drove along in silence for a while. About a mile from home, I caught sight of her bare foot thrust quickly between the front seats, precariously close to Ty's face. "How'd ya like that smell, Ty?" Tori teased.

"Get your foot down!" I commanded.

Ty backed away but said nothing. Very nice.

Tori obeyed, but continued to taunt her brother. "Ya know how foot smells, Ty? An' how cat poop smells? Good blend, huh?"

Ty giggled.

"Oh, Tori," I smiled at her in the rear view mirror, shaking my head. "You are such a naughty, naughty girl." We all laughed at the joke. She rushed in to clean up as soon as the car stopped, and all was well with the world again.

No complaints, no fighting, *wow*! Now that's what I call a relaxed attitude.

What Parents Can Do

- I handle stress by making jokes, and my daughter picked up that tendency. I'll admit it's not always the best way to go (during one C-section I had the anesthesiologist laughing so hard she didn't give me enough anesthetic), but I think my daughter used humor well in the situation above. Teach your children the appropriate ways to use humor:
    - The laughter shouldn't cause additional problems or diminish another person.
    - There is a difference between ridicule and good-hearted humor.
    - They can laugh at themselves, but never at the misfortune of others.
    - Learning to laugh at their own embarrassing moments can take the punch out of painful memories.
    - Humor should not be used to build themselves up at another's expense.
- Deep problems always need to be dealt with seriously.
- Require your children to treat each other well, but recognize when an unacceptable response is coming from fear or stress and grant a little leeway.

Prayer for Myself

Thank you for blessing me with children. Teach me the times I can ease up and just have fun with them.

Prayer for My Children

Give them relaxed attitudes that help them get through problems without overreacting.

Thoughts

The LORD observed the extent of human wickedness on the earth, and he saw that everything they thought or imagined was consistently and totally evil. So the LORD was sorry he had ever made them and put them on the earth. It broke his heart. And the LORD said, "I will wipe this human race I have created from the face of the earth."

GEN. 6:5–7

They think only about sinning. Misery and destruction always follow them.

ISA. 59:7

For as he thinketh in his heart, so is he.

PROV. 23:7 KJV

And we take captive every thought to make it obedient to Christ.

2 COR. 10:5 NIV

Whatever is true, whatever is noble, whatever is right, whatever is pure, whatever is lovely, whatever is admirable—if anything is excellent or praiseworthy—think about such things.

PHIL. 4:8 NIV

PERHAPS SOMEONE will argue that thoughts don't really matter, only actions matter. However, the Bible indicates if a person thinks about something long enough, he or she will eventually do it. People are what they think.

That's why counselors advise married couples not to think about divorce. If a couple decides they are committed to marriage, they will probably stay together. But if they allow thoughts of divorce to run around in their heads, the marriage is likely to break up. If a dieter starts thinking about the chocolate cake in the cupboard, she will eat a piece. If a young person allows himself to even consider cheating on a test, he will.

People eventually *do* what they *think*. Godly thoughts lead to godly actions; wicked thoughts lead to wickedness. Unfortunately, it is easier to think bad thoughts than good ones, and when a person allows his or her thoughts to run rampant, it results in a downward spiral. In Genesis, the earth had to be destroyed because of the combined evil thoughts of an entire civilization. It broke God's heart.

Fortunately, the Bible offers a way to avoid offending God with our thoughts. We are to "take every thought captive" (2 Cor. 10:5 ESV)As soon as we catch ourselves thinking negative, critical, sinful thoughts, we ask God's forgiveness and think about something good instead. That's it. That's the only solution. Focusing on good takes an effort of the will, but it is possible and the Lord will help us do it.

What Parents Can Do

- If you want to teach your children to think on things that are good and pure and trustworthy, let them see you concentrating on good things. They will be able to tell what you are thinking by what you say and do.
- Talk about good things with your kids to get their minds on a positive track.
- Encourage them by telling them the good character traits you see in them.
- Talk about the good in other people rather than criticizing.

- Since everything they see and hear influences their thought lives, monitor everything they look at, and don't be shy about refusing to let them read books and magazines that might cause them to think negatively.

Prayer for Myself

Help me gain control over my thought life by taking every thought captive all day long.

Prayer for My Children

Remind them you see every thought, and help them choose to please you by entertaining good ones.

Promises Kept

And because of his glory and excellence, he has given us great and precious promises. . . . In view of all this, make every effort to respond to God's promises. Supplement your faith with a generous provision of moral excellence, and moral excellence with knowledge.

2 PET. 1:4, 5

A man who makes a vow to the LORD or makes a pledge under oath must never break it. He must do exactly what he said he would do.

NUM. 30:2

The LORD detests lying lips, but he delights in those who tell the truth.

PROV. 12:22

A person who promises a gift but doesn't give it is like clouds and wind that bring no rain.

PROV. 25:14

GOD KEEPS his promises. Believing that and trusting him to fulfill his promises produces moral excellence. When parents are as good as their word, children develop character. But broken promises produce fear, hurt, lack of trust, anger, and bitterness.

Karen's father promised to pick her up after track practice her freshman year in high school. Three hours after the appointed time, the brokenhearted teen made her way to a pay phone in the school and called a neighbor to take her home. She was still crying when the neighbor arrived. Because Karen's father often "forgot" to keep his word, she struggles with bitterness and abandonment issues today.

Chad's dad gave "paper presents" instead of actual gifts. He would jot down the gift he intended to buy on the inside of a birthday card. Though he fully intended to buy the present, he would get busy and sometimes the gift never materialized. Other times bicycles would arrive six months after Christmas. Now grown, Chad cannot be trusted to keep his word. His character suffered as a result of his father's failure to keep promises.

What Parents Can Do

- Be as good as your word. You don't have to use the words "I promise" for your children to think you promised. So don't say you'll do something and then fail to do it, no matter how inconvenient it is.
- Be careful about saying "maybe we'll do it" when they ask for a favor. They likely won't hear the "maybe" part and will feel as though you've broken your word if you eventually decide against it. Instead tell them, "I'll decide later."
- Keep your promises quickly. Children wait in dog years; for every hour they spend waiting, they think they've waited seven.
- Hold your children responsible for keeping their word. If Josh says he'll take out the garbage as soon as he finishes his math, make sure he does it. If your daughter agrees to spend the night at Emmy's house, don't let her dump Emmy to go to a movie with Riley. Her word is her promise.

Prayer for Myself

Forgive me for the times I've let my children down. Help me see through my children's eyes so I recognize when something I mean as an offhand comment comes to them as a promise. Then help me keep my word despite the inconvenience.

Prayer for My Children

Make them people of their word who are diligent about keeping promises.

Manners

Stand up in the presence of the elderly, and show respect for the aged. Fear your God. I am the LORD.

LEV. 19:32

Above all, you must live as citizens of heaven, conducting yourselves in a manner worthy of the Good News about Christ.

PHIL. 1:27

Do to others whatever you would like them to do to you. This is the essence of all that is taught in the law and the prophets.

MATT. 7:12

MARY OWNED several valuable antique carpets, but was especially fond of the one in her dining room, which had been appraised at several thousand dollars. Her son's twenty-year-old college roommate liked it, too. On one visit to Mary's house he informed her, "When I get married I want you to give me this carpet as a wedding present."

At first Mary thought he was joking. When she realized he wasn't, she politely informed him she wouldn't part with her rug. The young man insisted. "You don't need it and I want it." The conversation ping-ponged back and forth with the fellow insisting she *would* give him the carpet. The situation grew very uncomfortable. Finally, Mary ended the discussion with an emphatic "No!" and walked from the room.

When that young man was little his mom never instructed him, "It isn't polite to ask for food at other people's houses." Because he didn't get that simple concept, he asked and even begged for things when he visited friends. That missing boundary led him to believe he deserved the belongings of others, and that taught him to covet. His mother did him a disservice by neglecting manners instruction.

What Parents Can Do

- Make sure your children never ask for anything when they go to friends' houses (except maybe a glass of water), but let them know it is all right to accept something offered by the host.
- Most manners are based on biblical values. In the story above, the young man was coveting, a definite no-no. His lack of manners revealed his lack of character.
- Usually good manners simply reinforce the character trait of treating others with consideration and not irritating them—the way you and your children would want to be treated (see Matt. 7:12, the Golden Rule).
- Teach them not to open the refrigerator in someone else's home.
- Tell them not to snatch things from children or adults, even if they just want to play with the item. Would they want someone taking their things?
- Make sure they know to keep feet off furniture in others' homes, even if you let them put their feet on your couch.
- Though it may sound extreme in today's culture, revive the lost art of good manners in your children:
    - Teach them to stand when older people walk into the room (see Lev. 19:32).
    - Insist they always say "please" and "thank you"; it's common courtesy.

    - Teach them to call adults by "Mr." or "Mrs." and a last name unless the adult gives permission to use a first name.
    - You might even go the extra step and teach the Southern way of answering "yes, sir" and "yes, ma'am."
- This list has been very brief. Buy a book on manners and teach your children how to behave. View it as a game; take pride in teaching them a skill; practice at home. Even if your children decide to forget about manners later, they will know how to behave. They'll know which way to pass the peas so they won't be embarrassed in important social situations; they'll know how to treat others with respect. And in the process, good manners will set boundaries that teach them excellent character.

Prayer for Myself

I've been tempted to neglect teaching manners because it takes so much time and energy. Please make me willing to pass along those skills to my children.

Prayer for My Children

Make them willing to learn manners. Train them to be considerate of others and respectful of the elderly. Teach them to behave in ways that make those around them feel esteemed and important.

6

Beautify the Rooms with Wisdom

"What lies behind us and what lies before us are small matters compared to what lies within us."

RALPH WALDO EMERSON

Obstructions to Forgiveness

O Lord, you are so good, so ready to forgive, so full of unfailing love for all who ask for your help.

PS. 86:5

But those who brazenly violate the LORD's will, whether native-born Israelites or foreigners, have blasphemed the LORD, and they must be cut off from the community. Since they have treated the LORD's word with contempt and deliberately disobeyed his command, they must be completely cut off and suffer the punishment for their guilt.

NUM. 15:30, 31

If you forgive those who sin against you, your heavenly Father will forgive you. But if you refuse to forgive others, your Father will not forgive your sins.

MATT. 6:14, 15

BRAZENLY CHOOSING to disobey God can also obstruct forgiveness. Greer met Joel at church, married him eight months later, and moved her children into his house. Before the year ended she caught him on the computer making arrangements to meet another woman. A couple from their Bible study took them out for dinner and confronted Joel about his adultery. Instead of protesting his innocence, he shrugged, saying, "God will forgive me."

Joel brazenly disobeyed the Lord and hardened his own heart.

A large majority of the seventh graders in the Christian school where I taught Bible admitted they would steal from their mothers' purses to get money to attend a concert even if they saw Jesus watching them from the doorway. It was no big deal because he'd forgive them, they said.

My seventh graders were in danger of hardening their hearts.

Once we harden our hearts, we seldom choose to ask the Lord for forgiveness, and he doesn't forgive unless asked. It's your job to impress on your children the dangers of hardening their hearts with blatant sin and the importance of keeping hearts tender by choosing to obey.

What Parents Can Do

- Lead by example.
- Always seek the Lord and be willing to obey him.
- Be very afraid to do anything that might harden your heart.
- Believe that any time you feel the need for God, he is initiating a relationship with you and will forgive you, even if you hardened your heart in the past, even if you've committed murder.
- Forgive those who hurt you.
- Urge your children to forgive people who hurt them and explain how to do it. (Read the rest of the section on forgiveness in chapter 6 for that information.)
- Tell your children to be very careful not to harden their hearts.
- God is always merciful and knows what is needed to soften hard hearts. Your continued prayers will open the channel for him to work in your children. Assure them that any time they feel drawn to repent and ask forgiveness, it proves their hearts have softened. God will absolutely forgive them.

Prayer for Myself

Thank you for forgiving me; nothing in the world feels better than living guilt free. I give you permission to do anything necessary to keep my heart soft.

Prayer for My Children

Guide them to want you more than anything else, and help them forgive the people who cause them pain.

Forgetting

I, I am he who blots out your transgressions for my own sake, and I will not remember your sins.

ISA. 43:25 ESV

Bless those who curse you. Pray for those who hurt you.

LUKE 6:28

ASK ANY ten people if they have questions about forgiveness and nine will ask, "Does forgiving mean I have to forget?" The answer is, since we can't just forget at will, no. I think the misconception that forgiving means we erase the event from our memory arises from the verse above. But the word *remember* (number 2142 in *Strong's Exhaustive Concordance*) means "to mention," "make to be remembered," "still think on," "record." God deliberately chooses not to mention our sins or even think about them. He will never "throw them in our faces." He keeps no records of them.

I wonder if it's because when he thinks about sin it causes him pain; you can see that clearly through the pages of the Old Testament. So for his own benefit, once our sins have been forgiven, he chooses to toss them away along with the pain that accompanies the memory. Plus, he refuses to cause us pain by jabbing us with accusing memories.

God is able to release the pain our sins caused him instantly and permanently because he's, well, God. But since we're human, forgiveness often comes in stages:

1) We are willing to forgive.

2) We ask God to forgive the offender just as Jesus did on the cross.

3) We purpose and choose to cancel the debt of the person who hurt us by releasing that person to God and refusing to retaliate for the wrong.

So why do we still suffer? Because sometimes forgiveness must be renewed many times a day for a long time. Jesus instructed us to forgive seventy times seven because the same offense can pop into our heads 490 times a day. And every time a painful memory returns, we must refuse to stew about it and choose to put it out of our minds by forgiving and releasing it to the Lord. Again. And again.

Gradually, the memory will return less often, and one day we'll be surprised to discover we rarely think about it. Better yet, when we do remember, there is no pain associated with it. That's when we know forgiveness is complete.

What Parents Can Do

- Give your children the "supernatural pain eraser": prayer for enemies. God commands us to pray for people who mistreat us (see quote above) because it helps us heal. As we pray for the happiness of the one who hurt us, he wipes away our pain. Plus, Acts 3:26 says God blesses people by turning them back from sinful ways. So a prayer for God to bless our offender is a prayer for that person to turn from wickedness.
- Teach your children to recognize unforgiveness in themselves:
    - Pain accompanying a memory should tell them they haven't totally forgiven yet and need to release the offender to God again.
    - Our forgiveness should mirror God's. Since he keeps no records of our wrongs when he forgives us, if we are keeping track of the times others hurt us we haven't forgiven them.

- Monitor your children to try to prevent them from forgetting without forgiving. Burying issues can cause emotional problems that burrow deep inside and bring severe problems later. For instance, kids who "forget" childhood sexual abuse can later suffer a variety of difficulties. If your child has been victimized, you and your child must face what happened, forgive the offender, and turn him or her over to the authorities for prosecution. Forgiving him doesn't mean he shouldn't be punished, and it's OK for you and your child to welcome the sense of justice.

Prayer for Myself

Help me forgive and pray for the people who hurt me; I know I can't do it without you.

Prayer for My Children

Protect them from deep hurt. Enable them to forgive people who cause them pain.

Bitterness

But when you are praying, first forgive anyone you are holding a grudge against, so that your Father in heaven will forgive your sins, too.

MARK 11:25

But if you are bitterly jealous and there is selfish ambition in your heart . . . Such things are earthly, unspiritual, and demonic.

JAMES 3:14, 15

See to it that no one misses the grace of God and that no bitter root grows up to cause trouble and defile many.

HEB. 12:15 NIV

Now . . . it is time to forgive and comfort him. Otherwise he may be overcome by discouragement.

2 COR. 2:7

RECENTLY I spoke with a friend who had not forgiven her husband for confessing he was attracted to her best friend. Though she knew he would remain faithful, she was devastated. It had been six months since the confession, and she had tried to forgive him, but finally came to understand she had not. She asked if I thought "things were getting worse" for her emotionally because she wouldn't forgive. I agreed that unforgiveness was causing her downward spiral.

Every time we refuse to forgive, even though forgiveness is difficult, there are consequences. God commands us to forgive; Satan says we don't have to. When we harbor unforgiveness we agree with Satan and not with God. Sadly, adopting the devil's attitudes allows him to get his dragon-claw into us, and with that toehold we have given him permission to enter our lives and torment us.

Unforgiveness turns into resentment; resentment makes us want to retaliate; retaliation grows into anger that builds to hatred. The end result is verbal or actual, physical murder. Our ruined relationships extend far beyond the initial hurt, and the only way to extricate ourselves is by doing what we should have done in the first place: forgive. Then we can heal.

What Parents Can Do

- Encourage your children to forgive immediately when they've been hurt. The sooner they can let go, the fewer problems they will have, and the more content they will be.
- If you can help your children understand Jesus' words on the cross, it may be easier for them to forgive. Jesus asked God to forgive his murderers because they did not know what they were doing. Obviously they did know they were murdering Jesus, but they didn't understand they were killing God, and they had no idea of the far-reaching consequences of their actions. In much the same way, no one who hurts us can fully comprehend what they are doing. They may not realize how deeply they hurt us; they don't understand they are damaging their own spirits.
- Encourage your children to forgive simply because God asks them to and they love him and want to please him.
- If they hold grudges, warn them how refusing to forgive can cause them problems.

Prayer for Myself

I hate it when my sharp tongue injures the ones I love. So often I speak sarcastically without even thinking about what I'm saying because the words are coming from a damaged place in my heart. Please forgive me and help me forgive others so I can speak life-giving words.

Prayer for My Children

Guide them to forgive quickly because they want to please you. Do that for their own protection, so Satan can never gain a foothold in their lives.

What Forgiveness Is and Is Not

Forgive us our sins, as we forgive those who sin against us.
And don't let us yield to temptation.

LUKE 11:4

Forgive others, and you will be forgiven.

LUKE 6:37

RUSS HIRED a Christian man from his church to remodel his house. Even though the man's work appeared shoddy, instead of firing him Russ tried to oversee the job more closely and continued to pay the man. Thousands of dollars later, with the remodel still unfinished, the man quit without notice and took Russ's expensive drill with him.

Needless to say, Russ was upset. That emotion rocketed to fury a few weeks later when Russ leaned on the second floor deck railing the man had installed and it collapsed. Russ caught himself just before plummeting headfirst onto the concrete ten feet below. The man's careless workmanship might have resulted in serious injury or even cost Russ his life.

Russ photographed the damage, intending to sue the man. A desire to teach the man a lesson ate Russ up for weeks before he decided he would have to forgive the man to save his own sanity—and because God commands forgiveness. Even though the man never apologized, Russ forgave the man from his heart.

In order to make the forgiveness stick, Russ chose to pray for the man every time angry thoughts of him came to mind. At first whenever Russ thought of the man, he prayed for the Lord to punish him; later he progressed to asking God to bless him. After nearly a year of daily prayer, all negative emotion disappeared. Today when Russ sees the man at church, he feels nothing but love for him.

Still, Russ would never hire the man to do another job, and they will probably never be close friends. That doesn't mean Russ hasn't forgiven him; it means Russ isn't foolish. The way the man treated Russ revealed the man's character and helped Russ know he wouldn't choose a relationship with someone who would act in that manner.

Russ knows forgiveness doesn't require or forbid reconciliation, and he understands that the man would likely disappoint him again given the chance. God doesn't expect us to knowingly place ourselves in a position to be mistreated.

What Parents Can Do

Help your children rethink some of the misconceptions they may have about forgiveness with these truths:

- Forgiveness means resigning their self-appointed role as judge by canceling the debt of the person who hurt them and allowing God, the only one who knows the offender's heart, to be the judge and deal with the person.
- They should forgive the person who offended whether that person apologizes or not.
- Forgiveness will free your children from the negative emotion and pain associated with holding on to hurt and anger.
- They need to keep forgiving as long as they continue to think about the wrong, even though they may have to forgive anew every day.

- Forgiveness does not mean they have to pretend the offender did nothing wrong.
- Forgiveness does not mean they are supposed to be doormats and allow others to keep hurting them. They should insist on respect for themselves.
- Forgiveness does not mean they have to be close friends with the offender ever again. They don't. But their attitude toward the person who hurt them must be good, and they must be able to pray for God to bless that person.

Prayer for Myself

In Jesus' name, I purpose and choose to forgive [name of the person who hurt you] from my heart. I cancel all [person's name]'s debts and obligations to me and ask your blessing on [person's name]. I ask you to forgive me for any bitterness or unforgiveness toward [person's name]. Holy Spirit, please heal my heart and show me your truth. (Based on a prayer from Wellspring Ministries, Anchorage, Alaska.)

Prayer for My Children

Help them fully understand forgiveness, and give them hearts to forgive the people who hurt them.

Integrity

Joyful are people of integrity, who follow the instructions of the LORD. . . . They do not compromise with evil, and they walk only in his paths.

PS. 119:1, 3

Even children are known by the way they act, whether their conduct is pure, and whether it is right.

PROV. 20:11

REMEMBER THE story of young Abraham Lincoln walking miles to repay a few pennies? Though many people would consider that debt inconsequential, Lincoln felt it was his responsibility to pay. Abe Lincoln had integrity.

While still a child, George Washington had too much integrity to lie about chopping down a cherry tree, even though the lie would have kept him out of trouble. I know some question the veracity of the cherry tree story, but even if it was fabricated to illustrate the first president's character, the point is the same: Washington was a man of integrity and everyone who knew him understood that.

We want God and others to recognize our children as honorable and trustworthy, but it takes consistent, daily work on our part to train them in the ways of integrity.

What Parents Can Do

- Integrity means following God's laws and refusing to compromise with evil. As you teach your children biblical principles, you will automatically build an understanding of integrity into them. The problem is, actually becoming people of high integrity is more difficult, since doing the right thing often conflicts with desires.

- As soon as they understand, begin teaching them to do right. Don't let your children get away with small things like stealing toys from friends or candy from the grocery store. Always insist they do as Numbers commands: "He must make full restitution for his wrong, add one fifth to it and give it all to the person he has wronged" (Num. 5:7 NIV).
- Teach your children that even though it will require courage, they must never compromise their principles. Not even when "everyone else is doing it."
- Situations that tempt your children to compromise will arise over and over in many areas. Continually reinforce the importance of behaving in honest, principled ways. Encourage them to take satisfaction in sticking to principles. Reward every upright action with praise and approval.
- Model integrity in every detail of your own life. If you tell your children not to steal, and then keep the extra change the cashier mistakenly hands you through the drive-thru window, they will learn integrity is situational.

Prayer for Myself

Open my eyes to see the little ways I compromise when I don't even realize it. Make me an honorable person whom my children would do well to emulate.

Prayer for My Children

Establish them as people of integrity who fervently desire to please you as they treat others honorably.

Judgment

Do not judge others, and you will not be judged.

MATT. 7:1

You can identify them by their fruit, that is, by the way they act. Can you pick grapes from thornbushes, or figs from thistles? A good tree produces good fruit, and a bad tree produces bad fruit. A good tree can't produce bad fruit, and a bad tree can't produce good fruit. So every tree that does not produce good fruit is chopped down and thrown into the fire. Yes, just as you can identify a tree by its fruit, so you can identify people by their actions.

MATT. 7:16–20

IN MATTHEW, Jesus first said not to judge. Then in almost the same breath he said to identify people by the way they act. Was he contradicting himself?

In our society, political correctness says if we label someone who has numerous affairs as promiscuous, we are judging. In reality, we would be correctly observing actions and applying the English word that fits. If Jesus didn't want us to observe the fruits of others, he would not have explained in detail how to do it. The last thing Jesus wants us to do is close our eyes to wrong actions; it is important for us to recognize them and know they are sinful. Only then can we avoid the same pitfalls.

So if observing isn't judging, what is judging?

Dr. James Richards explained in his book *How to Stop the Pain*, "The moment we judge *why* people do something instead of dealing with *what* they did, we have crossed the line into judgment. We have entered a place Jesus said not to go."

Judgment seeks a penalty; observation does not. Observation offers us two choices: We can either forgive the person or go to them with a loving attitude and confront the problem . . . without rancor and without attacking.

What Parents Can Do

- Use the Bible as a guide to teach your children to recognize sinful, wrong behavior.
- Instead of asking your children *why* they did something, ask them *what* they did wrong. Because *what* is an easier question to answer, it will start communication, and they are less likely to hang their heads in silence. Asking *what* also keeps them from making excuses and justifying their actions.
- After they admit what they did, ask them what they should have done. Surprisingly, most of the time they can and will answer that question.
- Discuss with them how they can implement a change and adopt right behavior.
- If the situation calls for it, set up a way you can check to make sure they do as they should in the future.

Prayer for Myself

Make me unafraid to observe and admit when I see sin in others or myself, but keep me from judging others by condemning them.

Prayer for My Children

Help them clearly see the difference between the commonly accepted societal rules of political correctness and God's rules. Give them the wisdom to observe without judging.

Kindness

But—"When God our Savior revealed his kindness and love . . ."

TITUS 3:4

Be kind to each other.

EPH. 4:32

MY CHEEKS still burn with shame when I remember my first day of high school. For some reason, Karen, one of the most popular girls in my class, had deigned to walk down the hall with me. I suppose it's possible she and I just happened to be walking the same direction at the same time so we fell into stride together. Still, we were actually strolling side by side, chatting. I was excited. Could this be my foot in the door with the popular crowd?

Then it happened. Charlene, the most reviled of all the school's outcasts approached. Alone, of course. She attended the church my dad pastored, and she'd expect me to say "Hi." I knew it. I averted my eyes and pretended not to see her.

I couldn't believe my ears when, just before I made it safely past her, Charlene said, "Hi, Jeannie." I ignored her.

Karen stopped right in the middle of the hall and stared at me incredulously. "Doesn't she go to your church?" she asked. My heart dropped.

There isn't space to tell you about all the tears I shed before the Lord that night or how I apologized to Charlene and became her friend from that time onward. Suffice it to say, that horrible glimpse into my character dramatically changed the course of my life. I made a couple of observations and decisions:

- I figured out popularity was not important.
- I realized everyone was shy, not just me, so I would make a practice of always smiling first and making others feel valued.
- I would never partake in cruel joking.
- I would not criticize others or listen when others were critical.
- In short, I decided to be kind from that day on.

Now I'm going to tell you something that may sound a little puffed up, but it isn't; I need to say it to conclude this story. In my senior year the student body voted me homecoming queen. Pretty amazing for a shy girl who never did achieve popularity and no longer cared about it. So why would my schoolmates choose me as queen? I was kind to them; that was all.

What Parents Can Do

- Remember kindness is one of God's character traits, and we should always emulate him. He's kind to you and your children; you be kind to others.
- Teach your children to be kind. Always. Not only will it make them more loveable, they'll have more self-respect.

Prayer for Myself

Make me the sort of person who makes others feel valued.

Prayer for My Children

Guide my children to have compassion and treat others with kindness.

Fill the House with Righteousness . . .

Hard Work

The lazy man is full of excuses.

PROV. 22:13 TLB

Lazy people are soon poor; hard workers get rich.

PROV. 10:4

Stay away from all believers who live idle lives and don't follow the tradition they received from us. . . . We worked hard day and night so we would not be a burden to any of you. . . . We wanted to give you an example to follow. Even while we were with you, we gave you this command: "Those unwilling to work will not get to eat."

2 THESS. 3:6, 8 10

Work willingly at whatever you do, as though you were working for the Lord rather than for people.

COL. 3:23

Never be lazy, but work hard and serve the Lord enthusiastically.

ROM. 12:11

AMBER ADOPTED a little girl from Eastern Europe. Not long after they arrived home, the two-year-old climbed down from her new mom's lap, toddled over to the shoes piled in a heap by the entry closet, and lined them up. The difficulties inherent in orphanage life had automatically offered the toddler a gift: She knew how to work.

It's more difficult to pass along that ability to children in our affluent society. We parents love to give them the best and do all we can to make them comfortable and happy. I plead guilty. That's not necessarily bad; it shows how much we love our children. Yet if we aren't careful, we can spoil them by requiring too little of them. Hard work is a skill that pleases the Lord and one we must pass along.

What Parents Can Do

- It's easy for children to make excuses, telling you why they don't feel well enough or are too busy to do chores or complete homework. Encourage them to "never get tired of doing good" (2 Thess. 3:13), and refuse to let them get away with slacking.
- Instead of sending them to do a chore by themselves, pitch in and work with them. Help make the bed; weed the flowers with them. They will learn to imitate your work skills. Besides, any job is more enjoyable when done with someone else.
- If they are having trouble in school, sit with them and help them as they study, but do not do the work for them.
- Keep your children busy. Our children each played a minimum of three sports each year, mostly because my husband is a sports fanatic who still plays basketball daily. But also because we read a study saying children who participate in sports earn better grades in school. And ours did. They learned to work as they gave their best efforts for the team.
- Encourage them to do their best at everything. Remind them they are doing it for the Lord, and don't get upset if work is not up to your standards. The important thing is for each child to accomplish commensurate with his or her own ability. If you demand more than your children are able to do, they will become discouraged and may give up.

- Expect them to handle a simple chore or two daily. They live in the house and should contribute to it.
- When they are in the middle of a sports season or getting ready for a play or recital, ease up on the expectations at home. Everyone needs a little down time.

Prayer for Myself

Help me evaluate my children correctly so I don't expect too little or too much from them. Show me how to pass along the skill of working enthusiastically.

Prayer for My Children

Guide them to work without being forced; teach them to enjoy hard work.

Strength and Courage

This is my command—be strong and courageous! Do not be afraid or discouraged. For the LORD your God is with you wherever you go.

JOSH. 1:9

Then David continued, "Be strong and courageous, and do the work. Don't be afraid or discouraged, for the LORD God, my God, is with you."

1 CHRON. 28:20

IN A LARGE Midwestern city on a summer evening, a woman whose throat had been slashed ran screaming for help toward my twenty-eight-year-old nephew, Adam Kinzinger. A man with a switchblade followed close behind her, intent on completing the job he'd started.

Adam remembers thinking only "This is gonna hurt" as he instinctively stepped between the two, wrestled the man to the ground, and knelt on the hand holding the knife. The man fought. Hard. Adam struggled to subdue him while shouting for someone, anyone, in the crowd of thirty onlookers to help. No one stepped forward. Several minutes into the fray, a passerby on a bike finally came to Adam's aid, and together they restrained the man until police arrived.

Though the woman required seventy stitches, she lived.

God exhorts us to be "strong and courageous," and there's no doubt my nephew was strong and courageous that night. But could Adam have subdued a knife-wielding assailant high on hatred, adrenaline, and drugs in his own strength? I don't think so. I'm confident the job was too big for Adam, and God stepped in to help. I don't know what methods the Lord used and Adam doesn't either, but Adam is confident he had supernatural assistance.

Whether or not your children will be faced with a physical confrontation as Adam was, they will certainly have to choose between courage and cowardice in other areas of life. Will they stay pure? Will they speak up when peers ridicule a classmate? I know you want your children to behave with courage and character.

What Parents Can Do

- Many times in his Word God exhorts us to be strong and courageous. Follow his example and tell your children often how important it is for them to be courageous, no matter what the consequences. Inspire them to do it because they choose to honor and please the Lord and because they want to help other people.
- Check your own attitude. If you would rather your children stay safe than act courageously, confess your selfishness to God and ask him to change your heart.
- When they do something courageous, tell them how proud it makes you.
    - In junior high, my shy son, Tevin, stood to his feet to speak in favor of waiting until marriage for sex, while the teacher and the entire class openly ridiculed him. I told him how proud I felt.
    - In elementary school, my son Ty protected a classmate when a bully attacked. The boy he helped had treated Ty badly in the past and did not thank Ty for the rescue. Ty's dad and I let our son know how proud we were.
- Teach them it's always worth it to be strong and courageous, no matter what the cost. If they suffer, it's for the Lord, and he will reward them.

- If your children are not courageous, address them as though they are. When the angel of the Lord found Gideon hiding from his enemies in the winepress, obviously afraid, he called him a "mighty hero" (see Judg. 6:11, 12). And that is exactly what Gideon became. When you speak positively to your children, your words often become a self-fulfilling prophecy.

Prayer for Myself

Help me care more about my children's character than I do about their safety. I accept the fact that danger may be involved when they act courageously.

Prayer for My Children

Please protect them as you shape them into strong and courageous people who please you.

Humility

Because of the privilege and authority God has given me, I give each of you this warning: . . . Be honest in your evaluation of yourselves, measuring yourselves by the faith God has given us.

ROM. 12:3

Be humble, thinking of others as better than yourselves.

PHIL. 2:3

So humble yourselves under the mighty power of God, and at the right time he will lift you up in honor.

1 PET. 5:6

HUMILITY IS one of the most misunderstood words in the English language. People mistakenly believe a humble person demurs when praised. A talented musician isn't supposed to realize he's good; a capable student should shrug and say, "There are smarter kids than me."

That isn't humility at all. A humble musician fully understands God has given him a gift and overflows with gratitude for it; a humble student recognizes God's intellectual gift and offers him glory for it. That is not pride.

In his book *Just in Case I Can't Be There*, Ron Mehl wrote, "Humility does not consist of focusing on what I am not. It isn't a matter of saying, 'Poor me. I'm nothing. I'm nobody. I guess I'll go eat some worms.' It is rather focusing on the might and greatness of God."

Humility is a choice.

Help your children recognize who they are and accept themselves, love themselves. God created them and loves them. It's not humility when they believe they aren't good enough; it's telling God he didn't do a very good job when he made them. That's a lie from Satan. They were made exactly the way God intended and, as the saying goes, God don't make no junk.

What Parents Can Do

- Teach your kids to humble themselves by seeing God, themselves, and others accurately without being prideful or critical. Show them to value others and put more importance on those people than on themselves (see Phil. 2:3).
- Let them know that when they do something well, it's OK to enjoy it as long as pride doesn't creep in. When complimented, they should say a simple thank you and feel grateful to God.
- Tell them humility changes to pride when they compare themselves with others less gifted than they are; it can lead to self-hatred when they compare themselves with others more talented than they. Neither is humility.
- Teach them to rely on God rather than themselves.

Prayer for Myself

Thank you for the gifts you've given me and my children.

Prayer for My Children

Teach my children to love and appreciate the way you've made them. Help them see themselves accurately, yet accept themselves, weaknesses and all.

Commitment

I, the God of Israel, will never abandon them.

ISA. 41:17

Even if my father and mother abandon me, the LORD will hold me close.

PS. 27:10

I will never fail you. I will never abandon you.

HEB. 13:5

His faithful love endures forever.

1 CHRON. 16:34

And I am convinced that nothing can ever separate us from God's love. Neither death nor life, neither angels nor demons, neither our fears for today nor our worries about tomorrow—not even the powers of hell can separate us from God's love. No power in the sky above or in the earth below—indeed, nothing in all creation will ever be able to separate us from the love of God that is revealed in Christ Jesus our Lord.

ROM. 8:38, 39

Commit your actions to the LORD, and your plans will succeed.

PROV. 16:3

YEARS AFTER a nobody-shepherd named David committed his life to the Lord, God explained King David's amazing successes: "I have been with you wherever you have gone, and I have destroyed all your enemies before your eyes. Now I will make your name as famous as anyone who has ever lived on the earth!" (1 Chron. 17:8). Because David committed himself so completely to the Lord, the Bible called him a "man after God's own heart" (1 Samuel 13:14). God orchestrated every triumph in David's life and made his name so famous we know it thousands of years later.

Do you want your children to be confident? Require them to memorize the verses above, because those verses will give them a firm grasp on the concept that the God who formed the universe is committed to them. He loves them fervently, always sees exactly where they are, and will always walk with them. Nothing can separate them from his love and protection.

Not only is God committed to loving you and your children eternally, God is committed to your success. But commitment goes two ways. If you want God's blessings you must commit your life to him in return. If you do, he promises to make you succeed.

What Parents Can Do

Start by teaching your children to:

- Commit to obey the Lord's Word.
- Commit to obey their parents.
- Commit to treat others with kindness.
- Commit to always keep their word.
- Commit to do the best they can at everything.
- Commit to allow God control of their lives and not get mad when he doesn't do things the way they think he should.
- Commit to wait patiently for him to act. (It was twenty years from the time God chose the boy as king before the man David actually assumed that position.)
- Commit to look for small successes and be grateful for them.

Prayer for Myself

Help me search the Scriptures to find the ways you want me to commit to doing and being. If there are areas of my life where I lack commitment, reveal them to me and help me become a committed, faithful person.

Prayer for My Children

Above all else, help my children stay committed to you their entire lives.

Church Attendance

> Have the people of Israel build me a holy sanctuary so I can live among them. You must build this Tabernacle and its furnishings exactly according to the pattern I will show you.
>
> EXOD. 25:8, 9

> "Every part of this plan," David told Solomon, "was given to me in writing from the hand of the LORD."
>
> 1 CHRON. 28:19

> For where two or three gather together as my followers, I am there among them.
>
> MATT. 18:20

ONE OF the first things God did after parting the Red Sea was to give Moses instructions for building the tabernacle where the Israelites would worship him. It was an opulent tent, and when the community moved from place to place, priests carrying it led the way. When they camped, the tabernacle was set up at the center of everything. That's how important God thought church was.

Later, God actually wrote down plans for building a permanent temple, the intricately carved walls of which would be overlaid with hammered gold. God commanded the entire population to travel to Jerusalem several times a year so they could all meet together and worship him there. Four thousand professional musicians were assigned to sing and play trumpets, harps, cymbals, and lyres at the temple whenever the community gathered to praise the Lord at those celebrations.

The sound of that four-thousand-person choir and orchestra praising the Lord must have been magnificent, awe-inspiring. That's church the way God likes it. And yet diminutive Chinese house churches must be precious to him, too, because he promises that any time two or three of his children meet to worship him, he'll be right there among them.

If the gathering of Christians matters to God, it needs to matter to your children.

What Parents Can Do

Right up front I need to tell you that not one of my children ever suggested staying home from church on a whim. Not once. They liked to go to church, and they still attend regularly. I'm not sure why they had such good attitudes, but I'll tell you how we handled it.

- I missed church on Sunday mornings only if I was really sick. The kids did the same. My husband missed once a month on National Guard weekends, but the children knew he had no other choice. That means we set an example of church attendance.
- The approach in our home was simply that missing church on Sunday mornings was not an option. I'm not sure I ever had to say it; they just knew it.
- Our only mandatory attendance was Sunday mornings, though they would often choose to attend other services or activities. During the rest of the time, all their religious instruction came from me. I focused on teaching them about the Lord to and from their regular school activities and sporting events as well as during evening chats.
- We searched until we found not only a church that my husband and I liked, but one the children enjoyed.
- Occasionally they would notice hypocrisy in someone at church. We would then discuss the fact that people come

to church because they need God, not because they are perfect. Their failure to measure up in no way reflected poorly on God.

I told you I never had a child who rebelled against church; now let me tell you what I would do if a child decided to rebel.

- First, I'd pray for wisdom and strength. I'd ask the Lord to make my child love worshipping with God's people.
- If he lived under my roof, I would insist he attend church, and I'd take away privileges until he decided he agreed with me. I would not argue about it, but determine in my mind that his staying away was not an option. He'd sense my strength.
- If my child argued he didn't need church to be a Christian, I'd agree. But I'd tell him God wants us to attend church because that's where we find others with God's Spirit living inside them. And Hebrews 10:25 commands us to continue meeting with other Christians.
- If I thought things might change if I found a church he'd like, I'd search until I found a good one where people brought their Bibles to service and I could feel the Spirit of the Lord.

Prayer for Myself

Give me wisdom to raise my children to love you and value worshipping with the body of Christ. Help me find great pleasure in corporate worship, and lead us to a church filled with your Spirit.

Prayer for My Children

Teach them to value the family of God and want to associate with people who love you. Give them a strong desire to attend church because they find you there.

7

Troubleshoot and Repair Substandard Work

"The measure of a man's character is what he would do if he knew he never would be found out."

BARON THOMAS BABINGTON MACAULAY

Fix Code Violations . . .

Dysfunction

> If we claim we have no sin, we are only fooling ourselves and not living in the truth. But if we confess our sins to him, he is faithful and just to forgive us our sins and to cleanse us from all wickedness. If we claim we have not sinned, we are calling God a liar and showing that his word has no place in our hearts.
>
> 1 JOHN 1:8–10

DR. PHIL AND Dr. Laura interview a lot of unhappy, dysfunctional people. Most of those people come from very troubled families, and though you're confident you personally shouldn't be categorized with them, I'll wager that at some point you've wondered about others in your family, right?

Especially your parents. We all wonder about our parents at times. They made mistakes and passed along quirks and ways of reacting that cause us and our siblings trouble to this day. Oh, they meant well, but deep down we wish they'd done things differently. Better. We hope to be an improved version of them.

And we can be. But it will take a lot of work, and it will happen only if we are willing to admit something none of us likes to admit: We *are* dysfunctional.

Dysfunction started with the first parents, Adam and Eve, and has to some degree infected every family and every human since. The word *dysfunction* simply means failing to function normally—the way God created us to function. Sin causes dysfunction because it is a corruption of the God-intended order of things. To the extent sin rules our lives, we continue in our dysfunction.

However, there is hope. By studying and following God's principles we can improve greatly. Proverbs promises, "The way of the righteous is like the first gleam of dawn, which shines ever brighter until the full light of day" (Prov. 4:18).

As our love for Jesus grows and we yield control of our lives to him, he will make us less and less dysfunctional and more and more healthy. The healthier we become, the stronger our character will be. And people with good character tend to pass those traits along to their children.

What Parents Can Do

- Since any dysfunction in you will certainly affect your child, be willing to look at yourself honestly.
- Every time you recognize a sin in yourself, do CPR: Confess, Pray, Repent.
- Read your Bible daily, and as you read ask the Holy Spirit to open your understanding. Learning from your Bible is the quickest, easiest way to improve character and become a better parent. Deal with whatever God reveals.
- Accept criticism without getting defensive. It is good to allow your children to tell you when your actions adversely affect them, but make sure they do it with respect. Ask God to show you if the criticism is true or false. If it's true, do CPR.
- If your children have seen your error, confess to them and ask for forgiveness.
- Forgive yourself when you sin. Since God doesn't belittle you but views you as his treasured child, why should you beat yourself up? Do CPR and let it go. If you have berated yourself for mistakes and sins in the past, ask God to forgive you, and decide not to do it again. Accept his forgiveness.

Prayer for Myself

Give me a willingness to look at myself through your eyes and confess and repent of every sin you reveal to me.

Prayer for My Children

Make my children emotionally, mentally, and spiritually healthy.

Self-Justification

We have built a strong refuge made of lies and deception.

ISA. 28:15

For you are the children of your father the devil. . . . There is no truth in him. When he lies, it is consistent with his character; for he is a liar and the father of lies.

JOHN 8:44

HAVE YOU ever known people who justify their actions? Every time you catch them doing something wrong, they offer a really good reason why they were forced into it. "I had to take money from my mom's purse because I didn't have enough money for that new top." "My wife would be wounded if she knew I download pornography. I need it because she doesn't meet my needs. I deny it to protect her." (That last excuse can make the self-justifier feel almost noble.)

Many people who justify their actions eventually believe their own press. People who self-justify seldom realize they are lying, because they are lying to themselves. Unfortunately, self-justification allows them to believe it's OK to do anything they choose as long as their motivation is good.

They began justifying behavior as children when their parents first asked, "Why did you do that?" That question inadvertently taught them, "If I can come up with a good enough reason, my parents won't think I was bad." That thinking is so prevalent in our society we even justify behavior in our court system. If a murderer has a good enough reason for killing someone, he just may go free.

People who make excuses for their actions use lying like a fortress to protect themselves from the disapproval of others. They don't understand that inside that fortress they are conforming more and more closely to the image of the father of lies, Satan.

What Parents Can Do

- Children justify behavior because they want approval. Guide them to understand that when we care more what others think of us than what God thinks of us, we are letting those people control us. Teach them to want God's approval without worrying what anyone else thinks. If they can develop that mind-set, it will give them freedom throughout their lives.
- Don't ask your children why; simply deal with the misbehavior. Make sure they understand it doesn't matter why they did it; it does matter that they not repeat the offense.
- Show them how they are lying to themselves when they believe there is any good reason for doing wrong.
- Teach them that excuses (lies) always make things worse. If they get caught, the lie combined with the original offense intensifies the hurt they've inflicted. If they don't get caught, their good character is diminished.

Prayer for Myself

Keep me from deceiving myself by making excuses for my bad actions. Help me hold my children to the truth when they attempt to excuse their own behavior. Give me the wisdom to clearly explain the dangers in excuse-making.

Prayer for My Children

Give them courage to honestly face the sins they commit, without trying to justify their actions.

Fear

There is no fear in love. But perfect love drives out fear, because fear has to do with punishment. The one who fears is not made perfect in love.

1 JOHN 4:18 NIV

For God has not given us a spirit of fear and timidity, but of power, love, and self-discipline.

2 TIM. 1:7

STRANGELY, THE opposite of fear is not security or acceptance or peace; it is love. When we are overcome with fear we have little room for love. Conversely, the more we are filled with love, the less space in our hearts for fear . . . because "perfect love drives out fear."

Fear protects itself; love gives of itself.

Fear hides from others; love reveals self and becomes vulnerable.

Fear demands we keep a distrustful eye on people; love helps us accept them despite their flaws.

Fear is concerned with what others think of us; love fills us with concern for them.

Fear neglects responsibilities; love pitches in and takes care of what needs to be done today.

Fear comes from Satan, but God *is* love; that's why love is stronger than fear. The Bible teaches that when you search for God with your whole heart you will find him. Inspire your children to seek God and his love.

What Parents Can Do

- If you are full of fear, you will pass that way of reacting along to your children. For their sake, you must work to overcome your fears.
- Ask the Lord to help you replace fear with the trust that comes as you understand how deeply he loves you.
- Deliberately choose to act in love by becoming vulnerable and revealing yourself to God and people close to you.
- Talk to a friend or counselor about the hurts that caused your fears.
- When you forgive the ones who hurt you and love them enough to ask God to bless them, your healing will begin.
- Choose to obey the words of 1 Corinthians 13, the love chapter, and pray for the best from others.
- As you overcome the fears in your life, you will be able to offer your children unconditional love. That love will protect them.
- Teach your children to concentrate on God's love and protection instead of fearing people and circumstances.
- Help them understand that the more they trust God, the more they are living in God's perfect love. And that is the love that drives out fear.

Prayer for Myself

I confess I need more love in my life. Please heal the wounds in my heart, and fill me with your love.

Prayer for My Children

Help me recognize places where fear may have already taken hold of them, and help me show them how to experience the love that can replace that fear.

Perfectionism

God's way is perfect.

PS. 18:30

Not a single person on earth is always good and never sins.

ECCLES. 7:20

For everyone has sinned; we all fall short of God's glorious standard. Yet God, with undeserved kindness, declares that we are righteous.

ROM. 3:23, 24

AT FIRST glance perfectionism seems like a good thing. It's wonderful to work hard at developing skills and doing things well. Shouldn't everyone have high standards? Don't all parents want to encourage their children to be the best they can be?

Absolutely . . . as long as they understand that perfection is impossible; anyone who strives to be perfect sets himself up for disillusionment. Only one person on earth has ever been or ever will be perfect: Jesus. The Bible makes it clear everyone sins, and sin is the opposite of perfection. If we think we are sinless, perfect, we lie to ourselves (see 1 John 1:8).

Perfectionism allows no room for failure. Because perfectionists believe Satan's lie that they have the potential to be perfect, even small mistakes throw them into self-condemnation and depression. Self-accusing thoughts play in their heads and lead them to hate themselves.

If you want your children to respect themselves and live contented lives, help them accept the fact that they will fail sometimes . . . and that's OK. God still loves and accepts them, and so do you. They need to forgive and love themselves when they mess up.

What Parents Can Do

- Encourage your children to do and be their best, but when they fail, insist they get right back up, dust themselves off, and learn from their mistakes (see Prov. 24:16). Help them understand mistakes are forgivable.
- Teach them that God works out all things for their good; he's so skilled at his job he is able to use even their mistakes. So instead of getting mad at themselves, they should give thanks for everything, trust him, and learn from their errors.

Prayer for Myself

Help me love and accept myself despite my mistakes, and show me how to make my children feel loved unconditionally no matter what happens.

Prayer for My Children

Help them understand and accept they cannot be perfect. Teach them to accept your unconditional love so they can pass it along to others.

Presumption

> The king appointed singers to walk ahead of the army, singing to the LORD and praising him for his holy splendor. . . . So when the army of Judah arrived at the lookout point in the wilderness, all they saw were dead bodies lying on the ground as far as they could see.
>
> 2 CHRON. 20:21, 24

> Paul lived and worked with them, for they were tentmakers just as he was.
>
> ACTS 18:3

> Work out your own salvation with fear and trembling.
>
> PHIL. 2:12 KJV

> Come close to God and God will come close to you.
>
> JAMES 4:8

TIME AND time again, the Bible demonstrates that even though God is the one who provides for us and fights our battles, he will always give us jobs to do, and he expects us to complete them. God fully intended to fight a battle for King Jehoshaphat, yet he gave the king two responsibilities: singing praises and marching to battle. The Lord provided for the apostle Paul and saved him from numerous dangers, but Paul still worked as a tentmaker to support himself whenever he could.

In his book *Ruthless Trust*, Brennan Manning called it "presumption" to assign our tasks to God. My pastor, Randy Remington, makes presumption easy to identify by offering a few concrete examples:

- The child who doesn't study for a test and then asks God to give him a good grade presumes on God.
- The woman who marries a non-Christian expecting God to change him presumes on God.
- The financially irresponsible person who expects God to fix his overindulgence presumes on God.

I've met more than one Christian who chooses not to read the Bible. They feel it isn't necessary because they can learn God's precepts in other ways. Maybe they can, but the information they get secondhand will always be imperfect. And when they don't spend time directly reading God's words to "work out their own salvation," they are presuming on God.

What Parents Can Do

- Since God already initiated relationship with your children, teach them to do their part by drawing close to him through prayer and Bible study. He'll always respond to them, but he wants them to desire him enough to seek him. That is their responsibility.
- Teach your children to pay close attention to what God is telling them to do and then do it.
- While it is important not to step ahead of God (see Isa. 30:1, 2), remind your children to be practical. If there is something they *can* do, they should do it:
    - Stay pure instead of begging God for a negative pregnancy test.
    - Hunt for a job rather than waiting for a phone call from a prospective employer who has no idea they exist.

Prayer for Myself

Help me consistently discipline my children rather than abdicating my role as parent and then presuming on you to shape them into people of character. Forgive me for the times I've neglected my responsibilities and asked you to get me out of a jam. Thank you for the countless times you answered that thoughtless prayer, even though I didn't deserve your mercy.

Prayer for My Children

Open their eyes to see what you want them to do, and give them willing hearts to work hard at the tasks you've assigned them.

Victimization

Now listen! Today I am giving you a choice between life and death, between prosperity and disaster.

DEUT. 30:15

Be strong and courageous! Do not be afraid and do not panic before them. For the LORD your God will personally go ahead of you. He will neither fail you nor abandon you.

DEUT. 31:6

How precious is your unfailing love, O God!

PS. 36:7

WHAT CAUSES someone to submit to abuse? The victim feels self-hatred and needs the abuse to reinforce his or her own lack of self-respect. He or she believes the cruel treatment is deserved.

It isn't. Victimization is a choice, and no one has to choose it. Nowhere in the Bible are we taught to submit to that sort of evil. We aren't to attack in return, but we must get away from the evil influence. If we allow the victimization to continue, we are saying the abuse is deserved. When we allow ourselves to be treated abusively, it becomes our sin.

What Parents Can Do

- Victimization is a choice. If you are a victim living in an abusive relationship, decide you deserve to be treated with love and respect. Don't respond in kind to your abuser by yelling and accusing him or her. Quietly command respect. Seek help from a pastor or counselor. You must stop allowing yourself to be victimized so your children won't imitate you and become victims.

- If you are an abuser, stop. Abuse is a choice. If you need help, see a pastor or counselor before your children emulate your bad attitudes and behaviors.
- Look in the mirror every day and tell yourself God loves you. Do it until you believe it. It's true.
- Remind your children repeatedly of their value to you and to God. If they understand how precious they are, they will not allow themselves to be victimized.
- If your child's dating relationship shows any evidence of verbal or physical abuse, help your child understand he or she is headed for trouble. Your child must break off the relationship immediately. Speak strongly on this point.

Prayer for Myself

Forgive me for the times I've hated myself. I believe that you love me and I am valuable. Thank you.

Prayer for My Children

Help them love themselves enough that their very personality commands respect.

Active and Passive Rebellion

Evil people are eager for rebellion, but they will be severely punished.

PROV. 17:11

No discipline is enjoyable while it is happening—it's painful! But afterward there will be a peaceful harvest of right living for those who are trained in this way.

HEB.12:11

THERE ARE two kinds of rebellion, active and passive. The active sort is easy to recognize: The child talks back or kicks his brother; he rolls his eyes when his parent speaks to him; he refuses to do his homework. If he's two he may hit; if she's sixteen she stays out past her curfew. Wise parents recognize active rebellion and deal with it immediately.

Passive rebellion is more difficult to identify. A child sulks or whines or "forgets" to stack the dishwasher several days in a row. It's easy to excuse the behavior because he's tired and doesn't really mean it. She pouted because her sister hurt her feelings, poor baby.

Please understand clearly: That behavior is rebellion and must be dealt with immediately, even if the child protests how unfairly you are treating him or her.

What Parents Can Do

- Be bold and discipline as soon as you spot rebellion; don't let it go for even a second.

- Set up consequences ahead of time and make the discipline fit the crime: "If you forget to load the dishwasher two times this week, you can add mopping the floor on Saturdays to your chore list this month."
- Consistently carry through with promised discipline. It may seem painful at the time, but your goal is to reap "a harvest of right living." You want your children to *do* good, not *feel* good.
- Discipline should come from love. Never humiliate, shame, or discourage your children. That will simply lead to more rebellion. Don't discipline out of frustration.
- Occasionally, either because you have grown accustomed to rebellious behavior or because you want to think the best of your child, you may fail to notice even active rebellion. Therefore, if someone you consider credible—maybe a teacher or a wise friend—suggests something might be going wrong with your child, listen and honestly evaluate what he or she is telling you.

Prayer for Myself

Grant me the wisdom to immediately spot rebellion in my children and the courage to discipline them appropriately.

Prayer for My Children

Keep them from active and passive rebellion. Open their hearts to accept the teaching I pass along from your Word.

Fix Code Violations . . .

Vengeance

> Dear friends, never take revenge. Leave that to the righteous anger of God. For the Scriptures say, "I will take revenge; I will pay them back," says the LORD. Instead, "If your enemies are hungry, feed them. If they are thirsty, give them something to drink. In doing this, you will heap burning coals of shame on their heads." Don't let evil conquer you, but conquer evil by doing good.
>
> ROM. 12:19–21

> Pray for those who persecute you!
>
> MATT. 5:44

IF YOUR son is old enough to walk and talk and reason a little, I assume you've taught him not to thump the kid who grabs his truck. And you've told your daughter it's not nice to pinch her little friend because the girl refused to play dolls. Good job. You've taken the first step in teaching them about vengeance: God says getting even is never OK. If your children understand that retaliating in small ways is wrong, they will automatically know to avoid murder. So your job is half done; that was easy enough.

Unfortunately, the job gets harder.

Sometimes retaliation is so subtle we don't recognize it as vengeance. Our spouse wounds us and we turn the cold shoulder. Or maybe we're simply a little quieter than usual; we respond with a restrained smile when he or she approaches. We tell ourselves we're acting that way because we're hurt, and we are. But it goes deeper. We're getting even by withdrawing love—just a little bit, just for a little while. We're trying to manipulate the person; we want the control that belongs to God.

God doesn't leave us without tools for handling those situations. We can turn to him for comfort and ask him to change the situation. He gives us permission to confront in love by saying what our spouse did that hurt us and how it made us feel, but we don't. We punish instead.

Once you learn to recognize subtle methods of retaliation in yourself, you can watch for it in your children.

What Parents Can Do

- Instruct your children vengeance is always wrong, and when they try to get even in any way, they are retaliating. Whether the person who wounded them did evil or not, when they retaliate, *their* actions are evil. They aren't responsible for the other person; they are responsible for their own actions.
- Point out obvious as well as subtle retaliation when you see it.
- Teach them how to handle wrong treatment:
    - Tell your children though tattling is wrong, it is *not* tattling for little ones or gossip for teens to come to you with a problem. God gave parents to children to teach them how to work through problems and to reassure them.
    - Show them how to turn to God for comfort.
    - Pray with them for the person who wronged them.
    - Encourage them to talk it out with the other person and make peace if at all possible (see Rom. 12:18).
- Let them observe you caring enough to stand up for them when they need support. If working things out between children may put your child in a worse situation, you may need to talk to the other child's parents. If you can't do that, talk to

school officials. (I once wanted to chat with the parents of the eighth grader who beat up my sixth-grade son in the locker room, but school officials wouldn't allow it.)

- Watch out for the self-pitying attitude that can precede vengeance.

Prayer for Myself

Even though getting even sometimes makes me feel better temporarily, help me not to fall into the temptation of taking revenge.

Prayer for My Children

Teach them healthy, God-approved ways of relating to friends and family.

Fix Code Violations . . .

Boasting

Their lives became full of every kind of wickedness. . . . They are backstabbers, haters of God, insolent, proud, and boastful.

ROM. 1:29, 30

How long will they speak with arrogance? How long will these evil people boast?

PS. 94:4

Let someone else praise you, not your own mouth.

PROV. 27:2

If everything you have is from God, why boast as though it were not a gift?

1 COR. 4:7

BOASTING IS a study in paradoxes. Braggarts sound arrogant and may actually be convinced of their superiority, but deep in their core they believe themselves inadequate. The haughty words mask a hurting center they may or may not know exists.

The purpose of boasting is to make the braggarts look good so others will be awed and approve of them. Instead, to people of discernment the boasting flashes "I am flawed!" like a neon sign over the braggarts' heads.

Subconsciously, the intent of braggarts is to think of others as lesser than themselves so they can feel good. Though they are usually successful in that, it causes problems for the boasters as well as for the people to whom they boast. The braggarts' arrogance hooks into the lack of confidence in others, and those people may feel instant disdain and hatred for the braggarts. Boasting actually blocks braggarts from the approval they seek.

What Parents Can Do

- Talk with your children about how hard it can be for any of us to keep from bragging, especially when we feel a little timid. Explain that the reason we brag is to make ourselves feel better. The remedy is to confess we are covering feelings of inadequacy and come to understand that what matters is our value to the Lord. Problems come when we love "human praise more than the praise of God" (John 12:43). If we can arrive at the place where we want to please God more than any human, we won't need to brag because we know he already accepts us.
- Teach them to recognize the causes of bragging without looking down on people who brag. Instruct them to treat those people with kindness, while refusing to feel put down by them.
- Explain to them the Lord calls boasting evil because:
    - Braggarts are trying to meet their own needs by creating their own feelings of importance. God wants them to look to him for their value.
    - Bragging reveals arrogance, which is pride. God hates pride.
    - Bragging hurts others.

Prayer for Myself

Help me recognize every time I start to brag, and to stop immediately.

Prayer for My Children

Take away their need to brag by showing them how valuable they are. Help them get their feelings of significance from you because they love you. Guide them to care more about what you think of them than what people think.

Manipulation

> But we have renounced disgraceful, underhanded ways. We *refuse to practice cunning* or to tamper with God's word, but by the open statement of the truth we would commend ourselves to everyone's conscience in the sight of God.
>
> 2 COR. 4:2 ESV, author's emphasis

> They are responsible to the Lord, so let him judge whether they are right or wrong. And with the Lord's help, they will do what is right. . . . Decide instead to live in such a way that you will not cause another believer to stumble and fall.
>
> ROM. 14:4, 13

SOME THINGS are so accepted in our society that few people even recognize them as wrong. Manipulation is one of those. It has been glorified on television and in movies since I was a child. Remember sophisticated and handsome *Maverick*-the-manipulator? Today the most "clever" manipulators win reality shows such as *Big Brother* or *Survivor*.

But manipulating is not clever; it is wrong. It is an attempt to control through cunning, getting our way by tricking others into doing or thinking what we want them to. Manipulating is wrong because control belongs to God, not us. When we manipulate others, we steal the free will God gave them.

Manipulation requires twisting the truth or outright dishonesty. Manipulators are never content, because they continually strive to make things go their way rather than trusting God to provide. Do your children know that?

What Parents Can Do

- It's your responsibility to point out to your children manipulation is wrong and why. As with every other instruction in right and wrong, you'll need to mention it every time you see it or hear about it.
- Children often try to manipulate parents. It starts with temper tantrums and progresses to more subtle teenage methods that are harder to catch; sometimes neither parent nor child realizes what is happening. Be on the lookout for those times, and don't allow your children to manipulate you.
- There is no need for you to manipulate your children. Tell them the truth about everything, and then pray for them to do right.
- If there is something you believe they should not participate in, have the courage to simply instruct them not to do it. Don't manipulate them into doing it your way. "Just say no" and stick to your guns. If it is nothing more than a gut feeling, tell them so; otherwise explain the reason for everything you do. That's how they learn.
- Choose to live by example rather than by manipulating. Otherwise, your dishonesty might place an obstacle in your children's lives.

Prayer for Myself

Forgive me for the times I try to get my own way by manipulating friends and family. Open my eyes to recognize when I am tempted to control, and help me repent and stop it before I even start.

Prayer for My Children

Help them to be straightforward and honest, living to please you and not trying to control the people around them.

Bigotry

Do not take advantage of foreigners who live among you in your land. Treat them like native-born Israelites, and love them as you love yourself.

LEV. 19:33, 34

Native-born Israelites and foreigners are equal before the LORD and are subject to the same decrees. This is a permanent law for you.

NUM. 15:15

My dear brothers and sisters, how can you claim to have faith in our glorious Lord Jesus Christ if you favor some people over others?

JAMES 2:1

God has no favorites.

GAL. 2:6

For he gives his sunlight to both the evil and the good, and he sends rain on the just and on the unjust alike. If you love only those who love you, what reward is there for that?

MATT. 5:45, 46

IS ONE race of people better than another? In the Old Testament, the Jewish race was chosen by God as his special treasure. Yet as soon as he led that race of people through the Red Sea, he made it clear he also loved the Egyptians traveling with them and the strangers living around them (see the verses above). God welcomed anyone who obeyed him. In the New Testament, our Lord had brown skin; a black man was given the privilege of carrying the cross for Jesus when he stumbled.

Doesn't God like Christians best? Of course God prefers for people to love and obey him and it delights him to bless his children, especially in answer to prayer. But he loves all humans and sends sunlight and rain to grow food that will nourish the good and bad alike. He doesn't show favorites.

Doesn't God look down on sinful people? Rahab, a forgiven prostitute, became one of Jesus' grandmothers. The genealogy of Jesus in Matthew lists her by name: "Salmon was the father of Boaz (whose mother was Rahab)" (Matt. 1:5). Jesus elevated the status of women, who are treated better in Judeo-Christian societies than in any other culture. Even modern societies such as Saudi Arabia allow men to marry four wives and refuse to let women drive.

What about children? Pagan people sacrificed their children to other gods; God condemned the practice. Jesus rebuked his disciples when they tried to keep children from flocking to him.

Are rich people better than poor people? In James, people who favor rich people because of their money are said to make "judgments . . . guided by evil motives" (see James 2:2–12).

The Bible views prejudice very simply: God has no favorites; he loves everyone. We're supposed to imitate him.

What Parents Can Do

- Our politically correct society is focused on racial prejudice. While it is never acceptable to consider one race superior to another, race is only one type of bigotry dealt with in the Bible. Watch yourself and your children for all sorts of prejudice. Are your sons chauvinistic? Does your daughter prefer friends who dress in name-brand clothes? Would you or your spouse prefer friendships with couples who live in expensive homes? That's all bigotry.

- Help your children understand that any person who quotes Scripture to "prove" his or her own superiority is diametrically opposed to God's truth. They are either misquoting the verses they cite or taking them out of context to make them mean the opposite of what God intended.
- Teach your children to not only treat those different from them with respect, but to ask God to help them love those people.
- There is a difference between caring about someone and choosing a close relationship with that person. As you teach your children not to be prejudiced against others, also remind them of the many ways the Bible cautions us to be careful in friendship. God's love should shine through you and your children to everyone; close friendships should be reserved for people of wisdom.

Prayer for Myself

Loving others is so hard for me; keep me from prejudice.

Prayer for My Children

Jesus, keep my children from prejudice against others, and protect them from becoming the victims of bigotry. But if they are ever mistreated because they are Christians, help them to welcome that bigotry knowing you will bless them (see Matt. 5:10).

Fix Code Violations . . .

Grumbling

Their voices rose in a great chorus of protest *against Moses and Aaron*. . . . Then the LORD said to Moses and Aaron, "How long must I put up with this wicked community and its *complaints about me*?"

NUM. 14:2, 26, 27, author's emphasis

And don't grumble as some of them did, and then were destroyed by the angel of death

1 COR. 10:10

Always be joyful. Never stop praying. Be thankful in all circumstances, for this is God's will for you who belong to Christ Jesus.

1 THESS. 5:16–18

Don't be dejected and sad, for the joy of the LORD is your strength!

NEH. 8:10

GOD TAKES grumbling personally. We may think we're grumbling about the job or the mother-in-law or the husband or a friend, but as far as God is concerned, he gave each of those to us for a reason, and we are griping at *him*!

The Bible instructs us to handle tough times by choosing to be joyful and thankful instead of grumbling. God tells us to pray when things go wrong and refuse to be dejected and sad, because our strength comes from the *joy* of the Lord.

What Parents Can Do

- Tell your children to choose to be joyful by thinking about good things and thanking God for them. God says that's where their strength will come from.
- Explain to your children that times may come when everything looks so bleak, all they can do is hang on to the fact the Lord loves them and will help them (see Hab. 3:17, 18). But if they do that and trust him, he'll restore them; they'll see him at work in their lives.
- If they can think of nothing good about their circumstances, tell them to think about God and his works in the lives of others or his miracles throughout the Bible. Tell them to read the passages about God's love and power and thank him for those. (Actually, I have a hard time believing God hasn't done *anything* to bless them. Unfortunately, sometimes older children stubbornly refuse to look at the truth. Instead of arguing with them endlessly, just offer that recommendation, and then go pray for them.)

Prayer for Myself

I confess there have been many times when I thought I was grumbling about others but was really complaining about you. Forgive me and open my eyes to the blessings you continually send.

Prayer for My Children

Help them open their hearts in gratitude to you on a daily basis. Teach them to view life positively and understand that every good and perfect gift comes from you.

Bullying

Don't rejoice when your enemies fall; don't be happy when they stumble. For the LORD will be displeased with you and will turn his anger away from them.

PROV. 24:17, 18

Do not seek revenge or bear a grudge against a fellow Israelite, but love your neighbor as yourself.

LEV. 19:18

Guard your heart above all else, for it determines the course of your life.

PROV. 4:23

DURING MY son's sixth-grade year, an eighth grader attacked him without provocation in the locker room. Though Ty had never seen him before, the kid approached from behind and slammed Ty's head into the metal locker. As Ty stumbled sideways, stunned, the bully continued to pummel him.

Ty's gaze slid around the twenty or so boys watching. "Anyone going to help me?" he asked, palms up. Every boy looked away, busily preparing for class.

Though Ty had never before (and hasn't since) been in a fight, he did play football. Using the hitting skills he learned in that sport, Ty drove forward, ramming his head into the guy's stomach. It took only three or four thumps for the bully to give up and leave. Bullies don't like people who stand up for themselves; it spoils their fun.

That evening, my husband and I gave Ty lots of affection and comfort, but neither of us reprimanded him for fighting in school since Ty obviously needed to defend himself. We did, however, monitor his attitude about the situation over the ensuing days and weeks, making certain that fear or the desire for revenge did not develop in him.

What Parents Can Do

- When the bully attacked my son, I went to school and addressed the problem with the principal and teachers. I suggested the locker room be monitored by an adult from that point on, and they accommodated my request.
- Make sure your child knows you are on his side and willing to do whatever necessary to keep him safe from bullying.
- Stay active in the school so you maintain a good rapport with the staff; it will make dealing with problems easier. It's not good to appear at school only when you have complaints.
- Since kids who are bullied tend to become bullies themselves:
    - We discussed the problem with Ty, making no bones about the fact we disapproved of the bully's behavior and stating it was apparent the boy had problems.
    - We told Ty how proud we were he would never bully someone, and we reinforced the importance of treating others with kindness.
    - We suggested he use the feelings from that situation to remember how it felt to be bullied. (Two of the character traits that mark Ty today are his kindness and willingness to stick up for underdogs.)
    - At the same time, we talked about the importance of letting anger go. We prayed for the bully together because the most important thing your children can do to keep from becoming bullies themselves is to keep their own hearts pure and free of bitterness.

- Never let your children bully siblings or friends.
- Sometimes older siblings take on an authority role with younger brothers or sisters; your children should all be equal and under your authority.
- As a strong adult, if you see any child being teased or bullied, put a stop to it. Immediately. Make sure all the children around you feel safe.

Prayer for Myself

I know a lot of adults bully others with snide comments or accusations or outright ridicule. Don't let me do that. I give you permission to call me up short any time I'm even tempted to be unkind, and give me the courage to apologize and change.

Prayer for My Children

Protect my children from becoming the victims of bullies. Even more importantly, make them so kind and considerate and protective of those weaker than themselves that becoming a bully is not a possibility for them.

8

Install Locks and an Alarm System

I have held many things in my hands,
and I have lost them all;
but whatever I have placed in God's hands,
that I still possess.

MARTIN LUTHER

Peer Pressure

Yes, I have sinned. I have disobeyed your instructions and the LORD's command, for I was afraid of the people and did what they demanded.

1 SAM. 15:24

PEER PRESSURE is one of the most insidious problems facing kids today, but there's nothing new about it. Fear of people brought about the demise of the reign of Israel's first king.

God sent King Saul to exterminate the Amalekites because they had fought against his people shortly after the Israelites escaped Egypt. God warned Saul to destroy everything—even the animals. But when Saul's men insisted on keeping the best sheep and cattle and everything else that appealed to them, Saul let them do it. He didn't want to displease them. He thought sparing a few cows was no big deal, but God rejected Saul as king that very day.

Giving in to peer pressure is always a recipe for disaster.

What Parents Can Do

- Parent confidently. Contrary to prevailing thought, children still listen to parents and want parental approval. Most of the time, your opinions will hold more weight with your children than the opinions of peers, even if it isn't apparent to you.
- Sometimes your children will *want* you to forbid them to participate in an activity everyone else is doing because they need someone else to blame for being different. (They may want

you to keep them out of sex education at school or tell them they can't go to a dance, and so forth.) That's OK. Just keep encouraging them to develop the courage to stand on their own.

- Your children will pressure you to relax rules you know are right. I can almost guarantee it. But standing firm is the unselfish way to parent because it proves you love your kids more than you care about their opinion of you.
- Continually talk about God's precepts with your children. Let them know you care fervently about their relationship with the Lord.
- Teach them to be willing to stand for right even if every one of their peers is choosing wrong. Tell them how proud you are when they choose God's ways.

Prayer for Myself

Help me cultivate a strong, loving bond with my children.

Prayer for My Children

Help my children want to please you more than their peers or me. Give them backbones of steel.

Movies

I will be careful to live a blameless life. . . . I will refuse to look at anything vile.

PS. 101:2, 3

CONTRARY TO the prevailing wisdom in Hollywood, G-rated movies are eleven times more profitable than their R-rated counterparts. So one might assume there must be more G-rated movies than R-rated movies produced each year. After all, everyone knows it's all about the money.

Maybe not. In June 2005 the Associated Press reported the statistic concerning G-rated movies mentioned in the paragraph above before continuing, "According to the Dove Foundation . . . the film industry made more than twelve times as many R-rated as G-rated movies from 1989–2003." I'm not sure how to explain that behavior from people whose supposed goal is to make money.

I certainly wish there were more G-rated movies produced, but these days even many G-rated cartoons are filled with empty values and peppered with sexual innuendo. I find it disappointing and shocking. And have you noticed the violence and nudity in PG-13 movies? As a parent, you need to put some serious thought and a lot of prayer into what movies you will allow your children to view.

What Parents Can Do

- Try applying the "What Would Jesus Do?" rule to your movie watching. Imagine Jesus sitting right there with you, looking at the screen. (He actually is, because he lives inside you.) If you think your movie would make Jesus uncomfortable, you shouldn't watch it, and neither should your children.

- Watch movies *with* your children and share your insights. Afterward, discuss what does and does not line up with God's Word. Closely monitor your children's viewing habits.
- Refuse to let them watch unhealthy films, even if they get angry with you. Pray they will still exercise wisdom about movies when they leave home.
- Pray for the people in media. Any prayer for them will indirectly benefit your child.

Prayer for Myself

Make me an example for my child. Give me the self-control to shun movies I would be embarrassed to have my children or Jesus see me watching.

Prayer for My Children

Show me how to teach my children to discern between uplifting and unhealthy films. Make them prefer decent movies and shun evil ones.

Television

To the pure you show yourself pure.

PS. 18:26

WHEN MY children were little, a cartoon called *He-Man* was all the rage. My kids *loved* it. But a Christian woman I respected warned me it was New Age and I shouldn't let my children watch. I didn't want to expose my babies to evil, of course. So I prayed about what to do.

Then I sat down and watched with them. Every time the hero would raise his sword and shout, "I have the power," I'd yell, "What's the sword?" And my children would cry enthusiastically, "The sword of the Sprit! The Word of God! The Bible!" I'd say, "Yes!"

When the skeletal villain appeared I'd shudder and ask, "Who does Skeletor symbolize?" (Yes, they knew the word *symbolize.*) They'd say, "Satan." And we'd all agree Satan was even worse than Skeletor and we wanted all evil defeated.

As a result, we enjoyed a rip-roarin' good family time every afternoon at four. I never did find out if the writers were New Age or Christian. It really didn't matter. Because we focused on the Lord, no evil thoughts harassed us as we watched.

What Parents Can Do

- Teach your children to evaluate every television show by the Bible's standards.
- Urge them to have the courage to turn off anything they feel is wrong.

- Keep petitioning the Lord to grant more influence to Christian writers and directors of television.
- Though there are a lot of cartoons and relatively harmless programs where you can still put my technique to good use, *He-Man* aired more than twenty years ago, and times have changed. If you have a question about a show's suitability, distract your children with other activities. I fully understand that keeping them from television will be a battle, but protecting their minds is worth the effort.

Prayer for Myself

Give me wisdom as I make decisions about what to allow my children to watch.

Prayer for My Children

When my children are confronted with lewd jokes or other evils in the media, help their minds stay so pure all the evil goes right over their heads.

Keep Out Intruders . . .

Video Games

> Be very careful, then, how you live—not as unwise but as wise, making the most of every opportunity, because the days are evil.
>
> EPH. 5:15, 16 NIV

SAM WORRIED about violence in video games. He watched his son carefully so he could immediately confront any violent behavior that cropped up, but the boy exhibited no signs of aggressiveness, and Sam thought he had the whole electronic game thing under control. He didn't. Danger sneaked in from an unexpected direction. The games stole the boy's time and motivation in much the way drug addiction would have.

In their book *Playstation Nation,* Olivia and Kurt Bruner wrote, "One out of four kids becomes addicted to computer and video games. And while many parents screen the content of games to protect their children from violent and sexual themes, few understand the forces causing their children to become hooked on 'the digital drug.'"

That's what happened to Sam's boy. The games were highly addictive, triggering physiological reactions in his brain in much the same way substance abuse would have. Even though he achieved more than many "game addicts" by graduating from high school and then college, he was content to return home and lounge on the couch, "gaming" while his parents supported him financially. The games dulled his normal human drives to marry or find a job.

What Parents Can Do

- Teach your children they are responsible to use their time wisely.
- I didn't understand the harm in video games when my children were growing up. I did make my older son change the demons into farmers in one game by removing their horns; I realize now that was a silly token gesture. If I had it to do over, I would refuse to let them play at all, even though I know keeping them from games would be difficult.
- At the very least, keep an eye on the video games your children are playing, and refuse to let them play harmful ones.
- After discussing the reasons for doing so with your children, limit time spent on games.
- If your children protest, tell them God holds you responsible to do what you think best while they live in your home. In a few years, they will be responsible directly to God and can do as they decide best.

Prayer for Myself

Show me how to direct my children to live purpose-filled lives. Then help me stand firm in a loving way if they complain against doing right.

Prayer for My Children

I rejoice in the bright future you have planned for my children. Teach them to use their time wisely.

Pornography

I will be careful to live a blameless life—when will you come to help me? I will lead a life of integrity in my own home. I will refuse to look at anything vile and vulgar.

PS. 101:2, 3

You can be sure that no immoral, impure, or greedy person will inherit the Kingdom of Christ and of God.

EPH. 5:5

So if your eye—even your good eye—causes you to lust, gouge it out and throw it away. It is better for you to lose one part of your body than for your whole body to be thrown into hell.

MATT. 5:29

ONE OF the sweetest young men I've ever known got hooked on pornography at age thirteen. His parents didn't pray against pornography because they never dreamed it could be a threat for their son. They were strong Christians who served as leaders in the church and thought they had protected him from catching even a glimpse of anything vile.

The boy gave no outward indication of a problem. In his teens, he read his Bible every day, participated in his church youth group, excelled as an athlete, and never stopped speaking up for Christ at school. His parents did not recognize anything wrong.

Yet pornography nearly ruined his life.

He couldn't escape its hold on him when he left home and attended a Christian college. It still controlled him after he married the homecoming queen. It lured him into an affair, where he contracted an incurable STD he will suffer from the rest of his life.

But once his sin was exposed, supported in prayer by his parents and friends, he sought Christian counseling and, with God's help, broke pornography's hold over him. He serves Christ victoriously today.

What Parents Can Do

- Even though pornography in books, magazines, movies, and personal computers did not exist when the Bible was written, there were other ways people could view vile things. Teach your children what the Bible says about pornography, starting with the verses above. Let them know Jesus was not speaking literally about gouging out eyes. People then understood those words as a way to emphasize how important Jesus considered "lust of the eyes." (If people from that era were to hear you claim someone "bit your head off" it might confuse them, too.)
- Role-play moral dilemmas with your children while they are very young so they will know how to react when confronted with temptation.
- Never give up hope, no matter how bleak things appear. God can rescue your children if you pray.
- Place the computer in a public area—family room, living room, and so forth, but not in a bedroom. Keep a close eye on usage, and don't leave your children alone with the computer for long periods.

Prayer for Myself

Guard me from neglecting prayer when it seems as though everything is going fine. Keep me aware and vigilant, knowing that my children need your continual guidance to guard them from unexpected sins.

Prayer for My Children

Protect my children from the dangers I can't see and can't predict.

Keep Out Intruders . . .

Violence

My child, if sinners entice you, turn your back on them! They may say, "Come and join us. Let's hide and kill someone! Just for fun, let's ambush the innocent! Let's swallow them alive, like the grave. . . . Come, throw in your lot with us; we'll all share the loot." My child, don't go along with them! Stay far away from their paths.

PROV. 1:10–12, 14, 15

Violent people mislead their companions, leading them down a harmful path.

PROV. 16:29

Now God saw that the earth had become corrupt and was filled with violence. . . . So God said to Noah, "I have decided to destroy all living creatures, for they have filled the earth with violence."

GEN. 6:11, 13

I GREW UP in Newcomerstown, Ohio, a small town so safe I could stroll alone on a starlit summer night without fear. But by the time I graduated from college and began teaching, the world had taken on ominous tones.

By the early 1970s, three of my affluent fifth-graders-turned-bullies students detained a classmate in the bathroom, punching him in the gut in imitation of a gangster movie they had watched the night before. Ten years later, a criminal my husband was investigating hired two hit men to kill our family. Five years ago, a man I taught as a seventh grader abducted and killed a young girl.

And the daily news proves violence continues to escalate. Recently, my harmless hometown spawned two killers who embarked on a murderous cross-country rampage.

What Parents Can Do

- Since violence begins in the heart, be a student of your children, quick to confront wrong attitudes and actions. Don't close your eyes to problems. It was obvious in elementary school that my student who murdered the child was headed for trouble. He bullied peers; yet when we teachers disciplined him, his father stormed to school and threatened us.
- Start early. Watch for any sign of potential bullying in your children. Don't let them hit, or even boss, siblings.
- If a teacher or trusted acquaintance implies your child has a problem, evaluate his or her words honestly and take the necessary action.
- Watch for the flip side of bullying: victimization. Children who are kind and shy can become the target of bullies.
- Work to instill self-confidence in your children since bullies are cowards and hesitant to attack self-assured individuals.
- Assess your parenting style; mocking, harsh parents produce insecure children who feel unloved and are easily victimized.
- To the best of your ability, keep them from vicariously enjoying violence in the media.

Prayer for Myself

Lord, help me understand that my children are in your hands; only you can protect their hearts, minds, and bodies.

Prayer for My Children

Place a quiet, gentle spirit in the hearts of my children. Give them compassionate hearts that keep them from violence. Teach them to carry themselves with the confident attitude that makes becoming a victim of violence less likely.

Illicit Sex

Can a man scoop a flame into his lap and not have his clothes catch on fire? Can he walk on hot coals and not blister his feet? So it is with the man who sleeps with another man's wife. He who embraces her will not go unpunished.

PROV. 6:27–29

And don't you realize that if a man joins himself to a prostitute, he becomes one body with her?

1 COR. 6:16

Don't fool yourselves. Those who indulge in sexual sin, or who worship idols, or commit adultery, or are male prostitutes, or practice homosexuality, or are thieves, or greedy people, or drunkards, or are abusive, or cheat people—none of these will inherit the Kingdom of God.

1 COR. 6:9, 10

ONE OF the biggest temptations facing humankind from the beginning of time is still its worst enemy today: illicit sex. Years ago the worship of false gods in the nations surrounding God's people centered on sexual orgies. The Israelites continually turned away from the Lord, at least in part, because they couldn't resist the lure.

That is one reason God compared Israel to an unfaithful wife: "Look. . . . Is there any place you have not been defiled by your adultery with other gods? . . . You have polluted the land with your prostitution and your wickedness. . . . Yet you say to me, . . . 'Surely you won't be angry forever! Surely you can forget about it!'" (Jer. 3:2, 4, 5).

God was angry. His heart was broken again, and he was forced to divorce the people he loved.

Illicit sex eventually causes emotional pain to the people who indulge in it. Victims suffer; God suffers; perpetrators suffer character loss and end up in hell if they don't repent.

What Parents Can Do

- If you have fallen prey to sexual temptation and your children know, admit that it damaged you, and urge them not to follow in your footsteps. If they don't know and aren't likely to find out, don't burden them with your failures. Just turn to God and do CPR: Confess, Pray, Repent.
- Know with certainty that failure does *not* disqualify you to take a firm stand on illicit sex. This isn't about you; it's about protecting your children.
- Protect them by refusing to allow impure books, magazines, computer connections, video games, movies, or television shows. And don't capitulate when your children complain loudly about your rules. Stick to your guns, or your children will suffer.

Prayer for Myself

Keep my thoughts and actions pure. Give me the wisdom and courage to set a good example for my children in sexual matters.

Prayer for My Children

Illicit sex is such a strong temptation, and I know my children will face it. Remind them the only way to escape it is to flee—to run away—from the temptation.

Books

For the foolishness of God is wiser than man's wisdom.

1 COR. 1:25 NIV

For as he thinketh in his heart, so is he.

PROV. 23:7 KJV

MOST BOOKS overtly or subtly reveal the worldview of the writer, because attitudes leak through no matter how hard the author tries to disguise them. The Bible says it best: "For whatever is in your heart determines what you say" (Matt. 12:34). That's why C. S. Lewis suggested more Christian authors should write secular books. He hoped their godly value systems would seep through and change the hearts of people who wouldn't even realize they were being influenced.

No matter what outlook lies behind a book, readers—including children—will hear it on either a conscious or a subconscious level.

Believe it or not, my dad loved the smell of skunk because of a book he read as a kid! At age eighty he no longer remembered the title of the book, the name of the author, or what happened in the story, but he continued to roll down car windows at the most inopportune times.

In junior high, Robbie stayed awake late into the night pouring through books written by existentialists and dissidents. The books magnified his already-twisted outlook on life, and his disdain for authority grew. In the eighth grade, he sneaked out of the house at three in the morning and exploded a pipe bomb he learned how to build from a book. He became a convicted felon at age fourteen.

Books influence kids. Never doubt it.

What Parents Can Do

- Don't trust a book simply because it is marked as a children's book.
- If possible, volunteer at your child's school. The reading series my children used in elementary school contained stories from several false religions. Strangely, since most people don't view other religions as "religion," the teachers saw those stories as nothing more than innocent narratives. If I hadn't spent time at school, I would never have learned about the reading series, and I would not have known to discuss with my children the fallacies found in the series.
- Read everything your child reads so you can maintain an ongoing discussion about the right and wrong attitudes present. (I know it's a lot of work, but you *can* do it.) It's best to read each book before they do so the two of you can discuss it as they read. Many of the best quality novels, most notably the Newbery Award books, are based on false religions.
- If you allow your kids to read the Harry Potter series, talk over every aspect of it with them. My daughter considered those books harmless until she worked at an institution for emotionally disturbed kids. Many of those teens followed the Wiccan religion. As my daughter learned the tenets of that point of view, she realized the Potter series is based on it in much the same way Christian novels are based on Christianity.
- If you see your children getting off track with their reading, don't be afraid to set them right. You're the parent.
- If they read something damaging, mitigate the damage by dis-

cussing the book in detail and giving them your opinion. They shouldn't mind. Most people like to talk about what they are reading.

Prayer for Myself

Help me find the time to read the books my children read. Keep me from being too rigid about what I allow them to read, yet open my eyes to dangerous influences, and help me explain them in ways my children understand. Guide me to say right things as I talk to them about their reading.

Prayer for My Children

Open their eyes to understand the value systems behind the books they read. Protect them from any evil they may stumble across. Teach them to desire healthy books.

Tools for Chasing Away Prowlers . . .

God's Armor

A final word: Be strong in the Lord and in his mighty power. Put on all of God's armor so that you will be able to stand firm against all strategies of the devil. For we are not fighting against flesh-and-blood enemies, but against evil rulers and authorities of the unseen world, against mighty powers in this dark world, and against evil spirits in the heavenly places. Therefore, put on every piece of God's armor so you will be able to resist the enemy in the time of evil. Then after the battle you will still be standing firm. Stand your ground, putting on the belt of truth and the body armor of God's righteousness. . . . Stay alert and be persistent in your prayers for all believers everywhere.

EPH. 6:10–14, 18

SATAN AND his demons are actual beings. Paul referred to them as "mighty powers of darkness who rule the world." It's important to believe they exist, because they are out to destroy humanity and if God's children sit back and do nothing, they have the power to accomplish it. They are the source of all evil, and they diligently work at destroying a child's character and turning him or her into a rebellious, godless person.

Fortunately, God provides supernatural armor to effectively fight against Satan's attacks. If we stand in Jesus' name using the armor, Satan can't defeat us.

What Parents Can Do

- Turn to Ephesians 6, and, as you read Paul's descriptions of God's weapons, spiritually dress yourself and your children with God's armor. How? In prayer, tell God you choose to wear the belt of truth, the body armor of God's righteousness, the peace that comes from the Good News about Christ, the shield of faith, the helmet of salvation, and the sword of the Spirit, which is the Word of God (see Eph. 6:15–17).
- Teach your children to put on the armor of God daily. Make sure they understand they may have to choose those weapons several times each day. For instance, if they are tempted to lie, they must choose truth every time they are tempted. Remembering the good news about Jesus will give them peace of mind when fear threatens. If they read the Bible, memorize it, and meditate on it, they can use it as a sword to overcome Satan by remembering Scripture when they have doubts.
- Over and over discuss with your children ways they may need to put on God's armor. Offer the armor as a possible solution whenever they come to you with a distressing situation.
- Talk about ways in which they can take the shield of faith by believing what God says instead of words spoken by teachers or friends. Act out putting on shoes of peace and standing firm.
- Stress that as long as they continue wearing God's protective armor, Satan will be powerless against them and they have absolutely no reason to fear him.

Prayer for Myself

Thank you for giving me spiritual armor with which to protect myself. Help me always remember that as long as I use your armor, Satan can't hurt me.

Prayer for My Children

Teach my children to believe that Satan exists, without focusing on him or fearing him. Help them remember Satan cowers at the name of Jesus.

Confession and Repentance

> We use God's mighty weapons, not worldly weapons, to knock down the strongholds of human reasoning and to destroy false arguments. We destroy every proud obstacle that keeps people from knowing God. We capture their rebellious thoughts and teach them to obey Christ.
>
> 2 COR. 10:4, 5

WHEN INDIVIDUALS choose sin, they allow the devil a place in their hearts. Each time they give in to temptation, his hold on them becomes stronger. The stronger his grip, the harder it is to resist him. Millions of people today are addicted to drugs, sex, pornography, gambling . . . and those are only the more obvious strongholds of the devil.

Most of people have at least a few strongholds they don't want to admit to. Many were well established long before birth and handed down through their parents (see Exod. 20:5). Typically, those are referred to as "generational sins," and they are some of the most difficult to overcome. Do you fly off the handle like your father? Make biting comments the way your mom always did? Do you hold a grudge? Nurse self-pity?

I may have missed your particular stronghold, but I'd be surprised if you don't have at least one. I do. Unfortunately, I've already passed mine along to my children, and if your children are old enough, you've likely already observed your "flaws" developing in yours.

Is there any hope? Can the cycle be stopped? Can the strongholds be demolished?

Yes! We can wipe out the devil's strongholds in our lives if we learn to employ God's mighty weapons of confession and repentance. As soon as we sin, we confess to God and anyone we wronged. Repentance requires change, so the next time we're tempted, we stand firm and refuse to give in to sin. If we fail, we start all over with confession and the determination to change.

It's usually a slow process, but eventually God's weapons will demolish the strongholds and we will have freedom. What a gift to give our children!

What Parents Can Do

- Ask the Holy Spirit to reveal sins you need to confess. Reading the Bible can help you spot them. Ask him to help you clear strongholds from your life so you won't pass them down to your children.
- If you observe strongholds in their lives, pray for the Lord to remove them.
- Talk to your children about strongholds. Explain what they are and tell them what God has to say about them.
- Teach them about God's powerful weapons of confession and repentance.

Prayer for Myself

Give me the ability to recognize strongholds in my life and the courage to confess and repent. Help me get rid of them so completely they won't be passed down to my children.

Prayer for My Children

Help me teach them how to confess and repent so they can destroy the strongholds taking root in their lives.

Praise

You have taught children and infants to tell of your strength, silencing your enemies and all who oppose you.

PS. 8:2

Shout joyful praises to God, all the earth! *Sing* about the glory of his name! *Tell* the world how glorious he is. *Say* to God, "How awesome are your deeds!"

PS. 66:1–3, author's emphasis

KATHLEEN SPENT years agonizing in prayer over a daughter who suffered from an eating disorder. God told her to stop worrying in prayer for the girl and simply praise him whenever her daughter came to mind. Kathleen obeyed and the situation started improving.

God instructed King Jehoshaphat to appoint a choir singing praises that would march ahead of his small army. He obeyed, and "At the very moment they began to sing and give praise, the LORD caused the armies of Ammon, Moab, and Mount Seir to start fighting among themselves" (2 Chron. 20:22).

When Paul and Silas praised in prison by praying and singing while the other prisoners listened, God sent an earthquake and released their chains (see Acts 16:25, 26).

Praising is one of the best ways to stop Satan in his tracks when you see him trying to destroy your children's character. If they will force themselves to begin praising when they feel upset or depressed or frightened, things will change. The enemies, Satan and his demons, are the ones causing the mental anguish (even if it seems to be coming from fellow humans), and praise defeats them. I don't know why praise works or how it works, but I know it does.

Praise is a powerful weapon, one that will lift your spirits and solve problems when nothing else seems to work.

What Parents Can Do

- Practice praising the Lord, and teach your children to use the weapon of praise.
- You don't have to use the word *praise*. Simply tell God about the awesome things he is and has done.
- Shout "Hallelujah!" It means "praise for Yahweh."
- Praise the Lord when you're alone (see Ps. 66:17).
- Praise the Lord as a family or in another group setting (see 1 Chron. 16:4).
- Offer a special gift to the Lord as a burst of praise. Leviticus 19:24 refers to a fruit crop dedicated to the Lord as a "celebration of praise."
- I believe most praise should be done aloud because most of the verses that urge us to praise mention praise that can be heard in some way. I wonder if shouted or spoken praise is a war cry that gives you courage to take a strong stand for Jesus in front of Satan and all his demon powers. Looking through the psalms you will discover many ways to praise. Following is a partial list:
    - Shout joyful praises to God.
    - Sing about the glory of his name.
    - Tell the world how glorious he is.
    - Say to God, "How awesome are your deeds."
    - Praise by playing musical instruments.
    - Clap to the Lord.
    - Make a joyful noise to the Lord.

Prayer for Myself

Jesus, thank you for giving me the incredible weapon of praise! Open my eyes to its benefits and remind me to use it daily.

Prayer for My Children

Teach my children to rely on the weapon of praise when they are depressed or feeling afraid or hopeless.

Shoes of Peace

> Then you will experience God's peace, which exceeds anything we can understand. His peace will guard your hearts and minds as you live in Christ Jesus.
>
> PHIL. 4:7

> For only we who believe can enter his rest. As for the others, God said, "In my anger I took an oath: 'They will never enter my place of rest.'"
>
> HEB. 4:3

I'D CALL myself an upbeat person. Oh, I have down times occasionally, but they're mild. God has blessed me and I know it. Recently someone told me I was "living the dream," and it's true. I love my life. I have a caring Christian husband, my children all serve the Lord, I live in a nice house, my health is relatively good, and I adore my job. So it only makes sense that I'd be happy, right?

Not necessarily.

I know people who have at least as much as I do (minus the Christian part) and yet battle inner turmoil. I've seen the faces of numerous others on television gossip shows and plastered across the front page of the newspaper. Furthermore, during the ten years I walked away from the Lord I was a mess, even though I looked cheerful enough on the outside.

Peace doesn't come automatically, but Philippians 4 gives several techniques for securing it:

- Rejoice always and be full of joy in the Lord.
- Don't worry about anything; pray about everything.
- Tell God your needs, and then thank him for all the things he's doing in your life.

What Parents Can Do

- Explain to your children the way in which God's peace works as a spiritual weapon. The hobnailed shoes Roman soldiers wore during Bible times gave them gripping power. The Bible is saying God's peace is like those shoes; it gives us stability, enabling us to stand through spiritual battles.
- Teach your children to choose peace by being contented with the things they have rather than always longing for something else.
- As you read through the Bible, list the things God says you need to do to dwell in his peace. (Philippians contains only a partial list.) Then do them and teach your children to do them.
- Remember God didn't promise we would never suffer or grieve or be hurt. He does promise to comfort us during those times, and it is possible to feel peace even in the midst of sorrow or suffering. Teach your children to ask for peace and expect it.
- Satan is your enemy as well as God's enemy. He can whisper accusing, despairing thoughts into your mind. It's hard to praise the Lord during those times, but force yourself to do it. Teach your children that praise defeats the enemy. It does (see Ps. 8:2). Once they defeat the devil with praise, peace will follow.

Prayer for Myself

Let my life be so filled with your peace that my children can see it on my face and hear it in my voice.

Prayer for My Children

Teach them to walk in your shoes of peace. Fill them with your presence, and teach them to praise you, thank you, and rejoice in your love.

Necessary Nagging

Therefore, I will always remind you about these things—even though you already know them and are standing firm in the truth you have been taught. And it is only right that I should keep on reminding you as long as I live. . . . so I will work hard to make sure you always remember these things after I am gone.

2 PET. 1:12, 13, 15

Consecrate yourselves, therefore, and be holy, for I am the LORD your God.

LEV. 20:7 ESV

I ADMIT TO feeling uncomfortable reading about all the perverse sexual sins in Leviticus. I couldn't understand why the Lord had to relay those unsavory details . . . until I read his explanation: "For the people of the land, who were before you, did all of these abominations" (Lev. 18:27 ESV). Since "everyone was doing it" God's people had lost sight of right and wrong. He was forced to explain to them exactly what was wrong and why. How else would they know?

In some ways, those off-base societies remind me of today. Many of our children have grown so accustomed to the seductive values of our culture they've lost the ability to distinguish right from wrong. Just as God did us a kindness by going into uncomfortable detail in Leviticus, we are responsible to explain to our children precisely what things are wrong and why. If you feel shy about it, go back and read all the things God says in Leviticus 18.

After you've imparted biblical knowledge of right and wrong, adopt the "nagging verses" above from 2 Peter as your theme, and sing the same song about right and wrong over and over. Keep nagging your children until you breathe your last breath. Don't forget to tell them your purpose: You hope they'll remember long after you're gone.

What Parents Can Do

- Never give your children more information than necessary, but if you see something needs to be explained, ask God for wisdom and explain it.
- Never stop reminding them how the Bible says they should live.
- Never stop telling them how much you love them and how much God loves them and how important it is to obey him.

Prayer for Myself

Help me understand your ways and correctly teach them to my children. I consecrate myself to be holy. Help me walk in your ways as an example to my children.

Prayer for My Children

Guide them and help them behave in ways worthy of you.

Ongoing Home Improvement . . .

Failure Is Repairable

For we are God's masterpiece. He has created us anew in Christ Jesus.

EPH. 2:10

This means that anyone who belongs to Christ has become a new person. The old life is gone; a new life has begun!

2 COR. 5:17

The godly may trip seven times, but they will get up again. But one disaster is enough to overthrow the wicked.

PROV. 24:16

I STUDIED OIL painting under Ann Ruttan, a nationally known landscape painter who occasionally worked on paintings for upcoming shows as the class painted. It was a thrill to watch. Her skill allowed her to whip up fabulous wall-sized oils with seemingly little effort.

But one day, after growing frustrated with a painting she had worked on for hours—one that refused to turn out as envisioned—she wiped a solvent-soaked rag around the canvas, leaving a dark, chaotic swirl that in no way resembled trees or flowers.

Ann stepped back, crossed her arms, and studied the disaster. After several minutes, she strode to the easel, turned the canvas upside down, and began painting furiously. The resulting masterpiece became the star of her next show . . . because the ruined mess underneath showed through the surface of the new creation, adding color and texture to the final work.

We make mistakes; our children will make them. But God can take our worst errors and remake our ruined life into his masterpiece.

What Parents Can Do

- Everyone fails at some time. While your children are young, instill confidence in them that nothing is ever so bad God can't redeem it.
- Remember and believe: No matter what they've done, how bad they've been, or how old they are, as you pray for them, God can change them into new people.
- Don't forget God loves your children, *no matter what*. Follow his example and love them unconditionally, too.
- Never let them forget God loves them. Always. Unconditionally.
- Teach your children to look at others with a compassionate, hope-filled attitude.

Prayer for Myself

Help me never give up on my children. Teach me to look at the good in them instead of focusing on their shortcomings. Grant me the ability to demonstrate unconditional love to them.

Prayer for My Children

Teach them an attitude of hope. Give them a deep understanding of you and your Word.

They Will Return

Direct your children onto the right path, and when they are older, they will not leave it.

PROV. 22:6

WHEN TELEMARKETERS call, I listen politely before explaining why I'm not interested in their product. Then, before the call ends, I ask if I can pray for them. I've gotten a variety of strange reactions, but one recent response outdid them all.

The call came just after lunch, when I needed a nap and felt too groggy to talk on the phone. Still, I felt strongly I should ask the question. So I did. "May I pray with you?"

The telemarketer at the other end, a young man named Dustin, yelled into the phone, "*What!?*" in a tone indicating he couldn't believe I would ask him something like that. I have to admit, it shook me a little, and I was tempted to hang up the phone. Instead I repeated the question.

Then I waited through a long pause before Dustin said in a small voice, "I used to go to church."

After a brief conversation, Dustin agreed to let me pray. I asked Jesus to bless the young man and let him feel God's presence and love. At the end of the prayer, Dustin added "In the name of the Father and the Son and the Holy Ghost" to my "In Jesus' name, amen." Then he confessed, "I was listening to bad music today. I knew I shouldn't."

He asked if intuition had prompted me to pray with him. I smiled at the grown boy's sweetness, reminded him how much

God loves him, and suggested he go back to church and start reading his Bible,

I think he will. I think his parents or a Sunday school teacher taught Dustin about Jesus at an early age, and God is calling the grown boy home so he can share a relationship with him and bless him. Don't you love the way God is working in Dustin's life? Isn't it great to know God can do the same for your children if they stray? Even if you don't know where they are?

What Parents Can Do

- Proverbs are general principles rather than specific promises. Still, if you train your children in God's ways and continue to pray for them, you can trust they will walk along God's paths as adults.
- Don't stop hoping and praying for your kids. God sees everything they do, and he knows how to bring them back if they stray. But he needs your prayers to open the way for him to accomplish that. John Wesley said, "God will do nothing on earth except in answer to believing prayer." The prayer is your responsibility.

Prayer for Myself

Show me how to teach my children your precepts. Let me communicate your love to them.

Prayer for My Children

Don't let them turn their backs on you. But if you do, I believe you will be faithful to bring them back.

Ongoing Home Improvement . . .

Hope for Parents Who Did Everything Wrong

I am about to do something new. See, I have already begun! Do you not see it?

ISA. 43:19

For nothing is impossible with God.

LUKE 1:37

The power of the life-giving Spirit has freed you from the power of sin that leads to death.

ROM. 8:2

I want to know Christ and experience the mighty power that raised him from the dead.

PHIL. 3:10

So God can point to us in all future ages as examples of the incredible wealth of his grace and kindness toward us, as shown in all he has done for us who are united with Christ Jesus.

EPH. 2:7

CAROLYN ROSE married young and converted to Mormonism to please her husband; he repaid her by abandoning her with four young children. Carolyn loved her children and did her best to raise them right, dragging them to the Mormon church every Sunday for years. But they hated it, and as a single mom she didn't have the energy to force them to go. Exhausted, she gave up on religion.

About the time her youngest son neared the end of his teenage years, Carolyn became a Christian. When she understood she had neglected the most important aspect of her children's education, she felt terrible. Because she hadn't taught them to accept Jesus, none of her children were Christians. Matt was an alcoholic who used drugs. The oldest, twenty-eight-year-old Janie, lived in another state, and Carolyn had little influence over her. It was too late. All Carolyn could do was pray and hope in God.

Then one day an *aha!* struck her. All her children owed her money and would go to great lengths to erase the debt, so she made an agreement with each. If they would go to church for a specified amount of time or agree to read the list of Christian books she suggested, she'd cancel their debts. What a deal! Each chose church. Within a relatively brief period, Carolyn's three younger children accepted the Lord, and Matt recovered from his addictions. Sadly, Janie still wasn't interested.

So Carolyn started sending Christian tapes to her oldest—and kept sending them, even though she knew her daughter wasn't listening. One late night when Janie was contemplating suicide, she glanced over and saw the tapes on her table. By the time she finished listening to them, she had become a Christian.

Today, all four children are Christians who can't say enough nice things about Mom. And Carolyn has several darling grandchildren. God is good.

It's never too late if you depend on the Lord for help. He can do the impossible, you know.

What Parents Can Do

- Carolyn had ingenious ideas that may or may not work for you. Ask the Holy Spirit to give you creative ideas tailored specifically for your children, but don't think saving them is up to you—especially when they are older. Convincing your children to accept Christ is the Holy Spirit's job. Yours is to be an example of a believer and pray continually for their salvation. Remember, the same power that raised Christ from the grave is still at work today.

- If the opportunity presents itself, explain to your children how to accept the Lord as their personal Savior and begin a friendship with him.
    - They must *believe* Jesus is the Son of God who saved us by dying for our sins, and they must *say it aloud*: "If you confess with your mouth that Jesus is Lord and believe in your heart that God raised him from the dead, you will be saved. For it is by believing in your heart that you are made right with God, and it is by confessing with your mouth that you are saved" (Rom. 10:9, 10).
    - Tell them they must repent; explain the meaning of repentance to them. Repentance means *turning* from sin and *obeying* Jesus. If it seems impossible to give up certain ingrained sins, assure them God will help them. He can even enable them to recover from addictions.
    - Guide them to confess their sins to God in prayer and ask him to forgive them. Assure them that as soon as they ask God to forgive them, he forgives. Everything. All guilt is gone.
- Encourage them to confess sins to people they have wronged and make amends when possible.

Prayer for Myself

Give me wisdom when I speak with my children. Help me not say things that irritate them, but instead rely on you to work in their hearts. Help me remain faithful by praying daily for them to come to know you. Give me faith to believe they will.

Prayer for My Children

I know you can work the impossible. Please reach into my children's hearts, turn them to you, and change their lives.

Ongoing Home Improvement . . .

Never Give Up

> As for me, I will certainly not sin against the LORD by ending my prayers for you. And I will continue to teach you what is good and right.
>
> 1 SAM. 12:23

THE WORDS in 1 Samuel 12:23 were spoken by Samuel the prophet. His mother left him at the temple to serve God as soon as she weaned him. After the death of his mentor, Eli, Samuel led the people of Israel for many years—until they rejected him by requesting a king to replace him.

He was hurt and disappointed, of course. He loved the people and wanted them to desire God. He knew a king would misuse his power to take advantage of them. But God reminded Samuel that the people were rejecting God and not the prophet, so after Samuel crowned the new king, he addressed the people one last time. He warned them to fear and worship God. Then Samuel reaffirmed that he would continue to pray for them and guide them, no matter what they did. God required it of him.

And God requires that you continue to pray for your children, no matter what they've done and no matter how they've disappointed you.

What Parents Can Do

- Never stop praying for your children. Never. Never. Never. No matter how old they are or what terrible things they do, God is faithful and can change them if you stand firm in praying for them. Remember, God can still work in your children after they leave home.

- If your child rejects you, remember he or she has to reject God and his instructions about honoring parents before rejecting you. That is heartbreaking but also comforting, since you and God are parenting together.
- Remember God is your child's parent and loves him or her more than you do. He'll never give up on your child.
- Never give up hope. God can still reach your child even in middle or old age. When I was thirty, my grandmother died with no assurance I would ever walk with the Lord. God answered her prayers and brought me back to him after she passed away.

Prayer for Myself

Make me faithful in prayer even when I am hurt or disappointed or disgusted by my children's behavior. Show me how to stand firm by continuing to teach and model right actions and attitudes, even if my children don't want to listen.

Prayer for My Children

Make my children grow into godly people who give you pleasure.

Ongoing Home Improvement . . .

How to Repair Broken-Down Foundations

Cry aloud; do not hold back. . . . Is not this the fast that I choose: to loose the bonds of wickedness, to undo the straps of the yoke, to let the oppressed go free, and to break every yoke? . . . Then you shall call, and the LORD will answer; you shall cry, and he will say, "Here I am". . . . And the LORD will guide you continually and satisfy your desire in scorched places and make your bones strong. . . . And your ancient ruins shall be rebuilt; you shall raise up the foundations of many generations.

ISA. 58:1, 6, 9, 11, 12 ESV

IT'S NEVER too late for children whose parents use the most powerful tool available: God-approved fasting. It can:

- Loose the bondage enslaving our children (see Isa. 58:6).
- Heal us and make us righteous (see Isa. 58:8).
- Ensure the Lord will answer our prayers (see Isa. 58:9).
- Give us guidance concerning how to handle our children (see Isa. 58:11).
- Satisfy our desire to see our children healed (see Isa. 58:11).
- Make us like a watered garden to them (see Isa. 58:11).
- Help rebuild the broken foundations of our children's ruined lives (see Isa. 58:12).

So what exactly is "God-approved" fasting? When I think about how God wants me to fast I usually consider two options: Should I do a "Daniel fast" and maybe give up lotions and chocolate or stop watching television for a month (see Dan. 10:2, 3)? Or should I stop eating food entirely for a period of time like Jesus did (see Luke 4:2)?

When Isaiah explained God-approved fasting, he didn't talk much about food; he addressed attitude and actions. You'll find some of the principles from that chapter below, but I can only touch on it briefly. Ask the Holy Spirit to open your understanding, and then read Isaiah 58 over and over for yourself.

What Parents Can Do

- Pray fervently.
- Be bold in telling your children where they have gone off track. A caution: Don't keep badgering them with it, but ask the Holy Spirit to give you wisdom regarding how to state it clearly to them. Once you know they understand, let it drop, and let your pleas and concerns ascend upward to God instead of outward to your children (see Isa. 58:1).
- Stop pointing the finger of blame and speaking ill of others (see Isa. 58:9).
- To the best of your ability, treat other people righteously. If you quarrel or are cruel, you are wasting your time fasting. God won't hear your prayers no matter how much food you give up (see Isa. 58:3, 4).
- Pray for bondage to be broken and the Lord to free your children from evil's grip (see Isa. 58:6).
- While you are waiting for God to answer, reach out to help others in need (see Isa. 58:7).
- Delight in the Sabbath (see Isa. 58:13).
- Now make a list of all the habits and addictions—"strongholds"—as well as the smaller sins in your child's life and use

that list to pray for him or her. Enlist three people who will entreat the Lord daily for your children. (They'll be more likely to stay faithful in prayer for your children if you also agree to pray for theirs.)
- Begin praising God aloud because you know he has the power to answer your prayers. Praise defeats Satan and can lift your spirits.
- Begin thinking of your child the way you would like him or her to be, and continually thank God he has the power to make that image become truth.

Prayer for Myself

I know the fervent prayer of a righteous person is very effective. Please show me how to pray effectively and fervently so my children will be healed and turn to you. Nudge me to pray every time they need an extra measure of help from you.

Prayer for My Children

In the name of Jesus and based on 1 Corinthians 10:3 and 4, I ask you to demolish the strongholds in [child's name]'s heart and life. Please show me every single sin that requires healing and repentance in [child's name].

[Begin to list every stronghold one by one, declaring the Lord is able to break them down.] Lord, please break these addictions and sins, and heal [child's name]. I believe you are strong enough to accomplish this. Increase my faith.

Appendix 1

Fifty Ways to Pray for Your Children

1. Sit in a chair with your thoughts focused on God's greatness, asking the Holy Spirit to remember your children as you meditate on him.

2. As you pray, cradle your open Bible, occasionally reading and meditating on the words, letting it guide your thoughts.

3. Ask the Holy Spirit within you to pray as you sleep. Then notice the worship songs and prayers that are running through your head every time you awaken during the night.

4. Fall to your knees, close your eyes, and speak aloud to God about your kids. Praying aloud with your eyes shut will help you focus.

5. Prostrate yourself on the floor or bed in the position of complete humility and submission as you pray.

6. Lift your hands as you petition him.

7. Each time you wake up in the night, pray for your kids until you fall asleep again; talk to God about them before you get out of bed in the morning.

8. In a journal, write out your requests word for word. Later record the answers to those prayers.

9. Make the most of your time by praying as you cook or scrub floors, letting part of your mind shoot requests for your children up to God as you chat with a friend, praying as you shower or jog, and/or praying as you drive the kids to soccer practice.

10. Write prayer needs on note cards and carry them with you everywhere you go. Refer to them whenever you have a spare moment to shoot up an arrow prayer, a quick request for help.

11. Meet weekly with a prayer partner and pray for both your children.

12. Read a written prayer. Let it prime the pump and encourage your own words to flow.

13. Just cry, "Help!" then wait patiently for the Lord to act.

14. Breathe one-sentence prayers for your child throughout the day.

15. Wrestle in prayer for your children by continually bringing your mind back to prayer when it wanders.

16. Type a prayer for your kids onto the computer as a screensaver. Every time you see it, pray it.

17. Fast to add power to your prayers; refuse all food for a few days, or determine not to eat chocolate or use lotions for a period of time.

18. Ask Jesus to help your children grow in wisdom and body and grant them favor with God and man (see Luke 2:52).

19. Pray daily for God to protect your children from disease, illness, accident, or permanent injury.

20. List every excellent character trait you see in your child, and thank and praise God for each one. Ask him to strengthen those traits and remove all unhealthy ones. Pray for the Lord to help you love your child perfectly despite flaws.

21. Turn to 1 Corinthians 13 and pray all those characteristics of love into you and your children. Ask God to make them patient and kind, not jealous or boastful or proud or rude. Pray they won't demand their own way, won't be irritable, won't keep a record of wrongs. Request that God keeps them from ever feeling glad about injustice, but makes them joyful when the truth wins out. Pray they will never give up, never lose faith, always be hopeful, always endure through

every circumstance. Pray that God will greatly increase his pure love in their hearts.

22. Ask the Lord to make your children wise in their choice of friends.

23. Turn to Psalm 139 and talk to God about everything it says. Thank God for choosing your daughter before the foundation of the world. Thank him for writing all her days in his book, for charting the path ahead of her, for scheduling good works for her, for walking ahead of and behind her. Praise him because he understands her so completely he knows every word she will say before it leaves her tongue.

24. Visualize angels with protective wings interlocked around your son as he walks and plays. Let your mind's eye fill that space with the shimmer of God's holiness.

25. Pray for a hedge of protection around your daughter, and imagine her future husband inside it with her. Ask God to keep them pure for one another as they grow in body and spirit.

26. Pray for kindness and consideration to fill your son daily; ask that the spirit of grumbling, backbiting, criticizing, and blaming stays far away. Ask the Lord to let your boy's uncomplaining spirit shine like the stars in the universe.

27. Request that bullies be kept from victimizing your children verbally or physically and pray that your children never bully anyone.

28. Ask the Lord to mold your children into people who love him with all their hearts, souls, and might. Pray for them to love others as much as they love themselves.

29. Ask the Lord to give them a strong desire to read and memorize his Word.

30. Pray for the Lord to make prayer a continuous happening in your life and the lives of your children. When they come to you with a problem, hug them and pray aloud with them even before you start to talk.

31. Pray for protection from sexual predators at school, on the streets, or in the family.

32. Tell God you accept everything he has in store for your children, but you reject every plan Satan weaves for them.

33. Pray for your children to develop a strong work ethic.

34. Pray for them to strive for excellence in everything they do so they can glorify God through their actions.

35. Pray for them to accept their own limitations when they try their best yet still fall short of their own goals. Ask God to show you how much you should or should not expect of them.

36. Ask him to give them strength to stand for him by making them as strong as a "fortified city that cannot be captured, like an iron pillar or a bronze wall" (Jer. 1:18).

37. Ask God to give your daughter a gentle and quiet spirit, keeping all crassness, hardness, and coarse joking far from her. Ask him to give her an innocence that shines forth like the dawn, a sweet spirit that announces her love for Jesus to everyone she meets.

38. Ask that your child immediately deal with hurt by forgiving rather than allowing it to escalate into anger, bitterness, and resentment.

39. Pray for your child's salvation. It is never too late to start. Even if your child is sixty and still unsaved, it is not too late to begin pleading with God to save him or her.

40. Envision your child cradled safely in God's hands; tell Jesus you know that is a reality, that he really does hold and protect your precious child.

41. Picture your prayers rising as a cloud of protection around them.

42. Visualize your child as a garden fountain, letting the pure living water of the Holy Sprit flow through him to water the thirsty people in the world around him.

43. When your child strays, ask God to allow your prayers to rip like lightning through the evil that envelops him. Ask the

Lord to let the searing fire of your fervent prayers open a path for God's Spirit and power to reach your child and heal him. Plead with God to lift the veil of deception from your child's mind. Pray for the convicting Holy Spirit to dog every step your son takes, whispering to him when he rises in the morning, stalking his steps all day long, convincing him of his rebellion as he goes to bed at night, waking him from sleep.

44. Pray for the Lord of the earth to make evil repugnant to your daughter. Ask for it to be a stinging stench in her nostrils that makes her want to vomit.

45. Ask the Lord to prevent you from getting in the way when he tries to discipline your daughter. Give Jesus permission to do whatever is necessary to get through to her.

46. Visualize your prayers floating up to God's throne room and mingling with other prayers in the gold bowls the elders hold in front of God's throne (see Rev. 5:8).

47. Close your eyes and imagine your child with the good character you wish he or she had. Keep that picture in your mind, and begin to thank God because you know he is able to change your child into that person.

48. Praise him because he sees your child every moment of every day; he knows exactly what your child needs even when you don't.

49. Thank God because he can do the impossible. Ask him to increase your faith until you actually believe that.

50. Praise God because he can change your child's heart, no matter how hard it is, because he is able to redeem the worst sins and make your child as pure as snow. Thank Jesus there is no condemnation for kids who belong to him (see Rom. 8:1).

Appendix 2

Memorize These Fifty Practical Passages from Proverbs

1. Don't even try to keep secrets from God; you can't.

"For the LORD sees clearly what a man does, examining every path he takes" (Prov. 5:21).

2. Trust the Lord to find God's will.

"Trust in the LORD with all your heart; do not depend on your own understanding. Seek his will in all you do, and he will show you which path to take" (Prov. 3:5, 6).

3. Ask for wisdom and God will give it to you.

"Cry out for insight, and ask for understanding. Search for them as you would for silver; seek them like hidden treasures. . . . Getting wisdom is the wisest thing you can do!" (Prov. 2:3, 4; 4:7).

4. Take every opportunity to help others.

"Do not withhold good from those who deserve it when it's in your power to help them. If you can help your neighbor now, don't say, 'Come back tomorrow, and then I'll help you'" (Prov. 3:27, 28).

5. Earn a good reputation and God's approval.

"Never let loyalty and kindness leave you! Tie them around your neck as a reminder. Write them deep within your heart. Then you will find favor with both God and people, and you will earn a good reputation" (Prov. 3:3, 4).

6. Don't destroy yourself by being cruel.

"Your kindness will reward you, but your cruelty will destroy you" (Prov. 11:17).

7. Be wise and be respected.

"The wise inherit honor, but fools are put to shame!" (Prov. 3:35).

8. Guard your heart.

"Guard your heart above all else, for it determines the course of your life" (Prov. 4:23).

9. Stop talking and listen.

"Even fools are thought wise when they keep silent; with their mouths shut, they seem intelligent" (Prov. 17:28).

10. Work hard.

"A lazy person is as bad as someone who destroys things" (Prov. 18:9).

11. Figure out if you're wise or foolish.

"Doing wrong is fun for a fool, but living wisely brings pleasure to the sensible" (Prov. 10:23).

12. *Live a long life.*

"Fear of the LORD *lengthens one's life, but the years of the wicked are cut short" (Prov. 10:27).*

13. Be honest.

"The LORD *detests the use of dishonest scales, but he delights in accurate weights. . . . Honesty guides good people; dishonesty destroys treacherous people" (Prov. 11:1, 3).*

14. Avoid pride.

"Pride goes before destruction, and haughtiness before a fall" (Prov. 16:18).

15. If you can't say something nice, don't say anything at all.

"It is foolish to belittle one's neighbor; a sensible person keeps quiet" (Prov. 11:12).

16. Don't gossip; be trustworthy.

"A gossip goes around telling secrets, but those who are trustworthy can keep a confidence" (Prov. 11:13).

17. Give generously.

"Give freely and become more wealthy; be stingy and lose everything. The generous will prosper; those who refresh others will themselves be refreshed" (Prov. 11:24, 25).

18. Take good care of your pets.

"The godly care for their animals, but wicked are always cruel" (Prov. 12:10).

19. Don't lose your temper.

"A fool is quick-tempered, but a wise person stays calm when insulted" (Prov. 12:16).

20. Choose wise friends.

"Walk with the wise and become wise; associate with fools and get in trouble" (Prov. 13:20).

21. Don't lie; you'll get caught if you do.

"Truthful words stand the test of time, but lies are soon exposed" (Prov. 12:19).

22. If you make a promise, keep it.

"The LORD detests lying lips, but he delights in those who tell the truth" (Prov. 12:22).

23. Think before you speak.

"Those who control their tongue will have a long life; opening your mouth can ruin everything" (Prov. 13:3).

24. Think before you act.

"Wise people think before they act; fools don't—and even brag about their foolishness!" (Prov. 13:16).

25. Don't believe everything you hear.

"Only simpletons believe everything they're told! The prudent carefully consider their steps" (Prov. 14:15).

26. Don't speak harshly.

"A gentle answer deflects anger, but harsh words make tempers flare. . . . Gentle words are a tree of life; a deceitful tongue crushes the spirit" (Prov. 15:1, 4).

27. Listen to your parents and get smart.

"Only a fool despises a parent's discipline; whoever learns from correction is wise" (Prov. 15:5).

28. Don't forget, God reads your thoughts and knows your motives.

"The LORD detests evil plans, but he delights in pure words" (Prov. 15:26).

29. Be successful.

"Commit your actions to the LORD, and your plans will succeed" (Prov. 16:3).

30. Be happy.

"Those who listen to instruction will prosper; those who trust the LORD will be joyful" (Prov. 16:20).

31. Encourage people with kind words.

"Wise words are like deep waters; wisdom flows from the wise like a bubbling brook" (Prov. 18:4).

32. Refuse to listen to bad words.

"Wrongdoers eagerly listen to gossip; liars pay close attention to slander" (Prov. 17:4).

33. Don't gossip about the flaws of friends and family.

"Love prospers when a fault is forgiven, but dwelling on it separates close friends" (Prov. 17:9).

34. Don't be rebellious.

"Evil people are eager for rebellion, but they will be severely punished" (Prov. 17:11).

35. Don't start a fight.

"Avoiding a fight is a mark of honor; only fools insist on quarreling" (Prov. 20:3).

36. Know where to go when you're in trouble.

"The name of the LORD is a strong fortress; the godly run to him and are safe" (Prov. 18:10).

37. Listen to both sides of a story before you make up your mind.

"The first to speak in court sounds right—until the cross-examination begins" (Prov. 18:17).

38. Don't be angry at God for something you caused.

"People ruin their lives by their own foolishness and then are angry at the LORD" (Prov. 19:3).

39. Obey God's Word.

"Keep the commandments and keep your life; despising them leads to death" (Prov. 19:16).

40. Be careful about loaning money.

"Get security from someone who guarantees a stranger's debt. Get a deposit if he does it for foreigners" (Prov. 20:16).

41. Never try to get even.

"Don't say, 'I will get even for this wrong.' Wait for the LORD to handle the matter" (Prov. 20:22).

42. Don't take shortcuts and do sloppy work.

"Good planning and hard work lead to prosperity, but hasty shortcuts lead to poverty" (Prov. 21:5).

43. Seek justice for the helpless.

"Speak up for those who cannot speak for themselves; ensure justice for those being crushed. Yes, speak up for the poor and helpless, and see that they get justice" (Prov. 31:8, 9).

44. Don't celebrate when your enemy gets into trouble.

"Don't rejoice when your enemies fall; don't be happy when they stumble. For the LORD will be displeased with you and will turn his anger away from them" (Prov. 24:17, 18).

45. Never go along with evil.

"If the godly give in to the wicked, it's like polluting a fountain or muddying a spring" (Prov. 25:26).

46. Practice self-control.

"A person without self-control is like a city with broken-down walls" (Prov. 25:28).

47. Don't brag.

"Let someone else praise you, not your own mouth" (Prov. 27:2).

48. Don't listen to flattery or flatter others.

"A lying tongue hates its victims, and flattering words cause ruin" (Prov. 26:28).

49. Obey God's law so he will hear your prayers.

"God detests the prayers of a person who ignores the law" (Prov. 28:9).

50. Don't fear people.

"Fearing people is a dangerous trap, but trusting the LORD means safety" (Prov. 29:25).

Bibliography

Adams, J. E. *The Christian Counselor's Manual.* Grand Rapids, MI: Zondervan, 1973.

Alcorn, Randy. *The Purity Principle.* Sisters, OR: Multnomah Publishers, 2003.

Bevere, John. *The Bait of Satan.* Lake Mary, FL: Charisma House, 1994.

Bruner, Olivia and Kurt. *Playstation Nation.* New York, Boston, Nashville: Center Street, 2006.

DiMarco, Haley. *Technical Virgin: How Far Is Too Far?.* Grand Rapids, MI: Baker Books, 2006.

Kendall, R. T. *Total Forgiveness.* Lake Mary, FL: Charisma House, 2002.

McDowell, Josh. *Evidence That Demands a Verdict,* Volume I. Nashville, Atlanta, London, Vancouver: Thomas Nelson, 1972.

Marsolini, Maxine. *Raising Children in Blended Families.* Grand Rapids, MI: Kregel Publishers, 2006.

Mathias, Art, Ph.D. *Biblical Foundations of Freedom.* Anchorage, AK: Wellspring Publishing, 2000.

Richards, James B. *How to Stop the Pain.* New Kensington, PA: Whitaker House, 2001.

Rigby, Jill. *Raising Respectful Children in a Disrespectful World.* New York, London, Toronto, Sydney: Howard Books, 2006.

Strobel, Lee. *The Case for Christ.* Grand Rapids, MI: Zondervan, 1998.

Taylor, St. John Jeannie. *How to Be a Praying Mom.* Peabody, MA: Hendrickson, 2001.

———. *The Guilt-Free Prayer Journal for Moms.* Chattanooga, TN: AMG, 2003.

Thomas, Gary. *Sacred Marriage.* Grand Rapids, MI: Zondervan, 2000.

Vandergriff, Steve. *Disturbing Behavior.* Chattanooga, TN: Living Ink Books, 2005.